FLIRTATIONS

IDIOM INVENTING WRITING THEORY

Jacques Lezra and Paul North, series editors

FLIRTATIONS

RHETORIC AND AESTHETICS THIS SIDE OF SEDUCTION

Edited by

DANIEL HOFFMAN-SCHWARTZ, BARBARA NATALIE NAGEL,
AND LAUREN SHIZUKO STONE

Fordham University Press   *New York 2015*

CONTENTS

ACKNOWLEDGMENTS

First and foremost we would like to thank each of our contributors, whose enthusiastic embrace of the topic has yielded a volume of essays in the spirit of flirtation. As many of the ideas and passages in this book are the direct result of a workshop held at New York University in 2012, we would also like to thank all those who participated in that conversation. The workshop was made possible by funding from The Humanities Initiative, the Program in Poetics and Theory, and the Department of Comparative Literature at NYU. The success of that event was due in no small part to assistance from Susan Protheroe, Brooke Baker, and Mari MacLean. The visual design that was used to promote the workshop and on which the cover of this book was based belongs to David Rager. We are particularly grateful for the support of Helen Tartar, and we are deeply saddened that she was not able see the book's publication. Thanks are due as well to Tom Lay for his work throughout the process and also to Richard Morrison for his support in the late stages. We are also pleased to thank the departments of Comparative Literature at NYU and Harvard for their financial support for the publication; heartfelt thanks as well to Jacques Lezra and especially John Hamilton, who championed this project from its earliest stages. Finally, we would also like to thank Paul North and (again) Jacques Lezra, for their inclusion of this work in their "Idiom" series, a context that perfectly suits the spirit of *Flirtations*.

FLIRTATIONS

"ALMOST NOTHING; ALMOST EVERYTHING": AN INTRODUCTION TO THE DISCOURSE OF FLIRTATION

Daniel Hoffman-Schwartz
Barbara Natalie Nagel
Lauren Shizuko Stone

What is flirtation, and how does it differ from seduction? The essays collected in this volume address the relatively undertheorized terrain of flirtation not as a subgenre of seduction but as a phenomenon in its own right. Indeed, in historical terms the particular question of flirtation has tended to be obscured by that of seduction, which has understandably been a major preoccupation for twentieth-century thought and critical theory. The discourse of seduction and the critique of seduction are unified by their shared obsession with a very determinate end: power. Flirtation, by contrast, is a game in which no one seems to gain the upper hand and no one seems to surrender.

Our topic is not an entirely novel one. The point rather is to reconstruct and reactivate a counterdiscourse that has been hiding in plain sight all along, adjacent to (and no doubt sometimes overlapping with) the more spectacular discourse of seduction. Though flirtation and theory share a long history, perhaps dating back to Plato's

Symposium, this countertradition comes into particular focus in European thought in the first half of the twentieth century; it is informed positively by the new philosophical interest in everyday life and informed negatively by the emergent politics of mass seduction.[1] Points of reference throughout this anthology thus include the thought-images (*Denkbilder*) and aphorisms of the Frankfurt School, Heidegger's conceptualization of "everydayness" (*Alltäglichkeit*), Freudian psychoanalysis, and the avant-garde *sociologie* of Caillois and Bataille.[2] If, however, we were to select a single text as the point of departure for this volume, it would be Georg Simmel's seminal 1909 essay, "Flirtation" ("Die Koketterie"), which presents flirtation as a paradigmatic theoretical topos for modernity itself. [3]

Simmel's analysis is remarkable for, among other reasons, the analogy it proposes between flirtation and aesthetic experience, the latter characterized as "purposiveness without purpose" in the famous Kantian formula that Simmel cites.[4] Although there is thus an aesthetic dimension to Simmel's extremely rich analysis, it is limited to an investigation of the vernacular aesthetics of urban life: He does not touch on the representation of flirtation in works of art or literature, nor does he make any broader claims about an affinity between flirtation and the field of aesthetics as such.

Simmel's student Ernst Bloch picks up on the topic of flirtation as well as on the Simmelian form of the thought-image in his short essay "Pippa Passes" ("Pippa geht vorüber") from the magnificent collection *Traces* (*Spuren*).[5] Yet unlike his teacher, Bloch allows his essay to leave behind the descriptive in order to get carried away in a more poetic—if not utopian—direction: "It's terrible to be misled too little, and yet just enough. Not much more than a twinkling arises, short and sharp, that wounds. It excites and may well sow something, but only beginnings,—nothing that blooms or could ever come to bloom."[6] It is the many interruptions in the narration, the "failure" to tell a teleological story in a straightforward fashion, that show what flirtation appears to be for Bloch: the wanderings of the *flâneur*,

Baudelaire's "À une passante," an everyday art of failing, of embracing the bygone. To quote Bloch again: "Striking, how seldom the joys of the bygone are described, and how reluctantly."[7] The narrator of "Pippa Passes" tells the story of a friend who meets a girl on a bus in Paris, first hardly noticing her. Then, by accident, he touches her leg—and is amused to think that she took him for someone hitting on her in a rather aggressive manner. She turns away, thus releasing him from the not so chivalrous obligation of having to reject her. The young man gets off the bus lightheartedly. But then the real failure occurs: "Love exploded on a time fuse,"[8] and suddenly, deplorably, he covets the woman; he succumbs to the capitalistic urge to possess what can be enjoyed only in passing. For Bloch flirtation requires a delicate economy of "almost-nothing, almost-everything."[9] It is this approach that critical theory takes toward flirtation and on which we reflect in this anthology: the hope for a mode of encounter that succeeds in failing and fails in succeeding.

"We are at our most transgressive when we fail,"[10] states Adam Phillips in his collection of essays, *On Flirtation*. Psychoanalytically oriented, it is the most celebrated recent work on the topic;[11] Phillips names Simmel as one of its main interlocutors. Flirtation for Phillips is tied to failure and transgression because it produces uncertainty, and hence presents "an often unconscious form of skepticism."[12] Phillips treats flirtation less as a given object and more as a mode, practice, or style; the introduction and two essays deal with flirtation and (Freud's theory of) seduction in a thematic manner, and the remaining essays treat it as a particular mode of engagement. "Contingency for beginners" is what Phillips calls flirtation: "It eroticizes the contingency of our lives by turning doubt—or ambiguity—into suspense."[13] On account of its epistemological uncertainty, flirtation sometimes triggers suspense that can become so intense as to appear to be "sadomasochism with a light touch"[14]—transgressive indeed. For all of its marvelous literariness, *On Flirtation* still falls squarely in the domain of psychoanalytic theory and practice.

The current volume draws on the interdisciplinary history of scholarship on flirtation even as it approaches the question from a distinctly aesthetic and literary-theoretical point of view. The essays give an account of the practice of flirtation and of the figure of the flirt as seen through the lenses of aesthetics and literary theory, exploring flirtation's involvement with issues of mimesis, poetic ambiguity, and indeed something akin to aesthetic pleasure. Moreover, in bringing the topos of flirtation into view, the readings reveal it as a form of literary self-reflection: Literature seems to talk about itself when it talks about flirtation. In what remains of this introduction we will turn to a few other key theoretical frames for the project with particular regard to the literariness of flirtation and its implications for the form of the volume itself before previewing the actual essays.

Can one flirt alone? Intuitively the answer would most likely be no—and thus the format of this book, like the structure of play itself, provides the flirt with one who flirts back. As a figure, flirtation has a dance-like quality and therefore needs an Other who takes up the movement and responds to the gesture. We begin by drawing on Roland Barthes's dramatic method and choreographic use of *figures* (in *A Lover's Discourse*) as something "that has been read, heard, felt. . . . A figure is established if at least someone can say: *'That's so true! I recognize that scene of language.'*"[15] But unlike Barthes's lover in solitude, who is "confronting the other . . . , who does not speak,"[16] flirtation can be sustained only if an Other plays along. In effect the flirting parties always perform a sort of dialogue. We have therefore chosen to present six short flirtations between two subjects of writing, one initiating the flirt and the other responding to it. The dialogic principle in this anthology recalls the *Symposium*, which poses the question of whether Platonic dialogues partake in a form of flirtation and what it would mean to recast the love of wisdom (*philosophia*) as a playful and possibly pointless chase.

Twentieth-century philosophy has learned much from interrogating this ancient form. Stanley Cavell's project in his classic *Pursuits of Happiness: The Hollywood Comedy of Remarriage* has numerous points of overlap with our own, most emphatically in the affinity he points to between criticism and conversation. His own essays double this figure of discourse: in Cavell's words, criticism is "a natural extension of conversation," and the films he writes on "are themselves investigations of (parts of a conversation about) ideas of conversation."[17] Cavell implicitly places his dialogue-heavy comedies of remarriage in the lineage of the *Symposium*. Looking back to the early days of sound cinema, his comedies mark a kind of rupture with the predominantly visual and gestural logic of flirtation associated with discourses of modernity and the city from Baudelaire to Simmel. "What does a happy marriage *sound* like?"[18] asks Cavell, hinting at the reinscription of philosophical dialogue within the new, intensively auditory medial atmosphere of sound cinema.[19]

Do married couples flirt? What about couples on the way to remarriage? What can we learn from Cavell about flirtation? And what do we learn from focusing on flirtation rather than marriage? To quote Cavell again: "In those films, talking together is plainly and fully being together, a mode of association, a form of life, and I would like to say that in these films the central pair are learning to speak the same language."[20] Perhaps Cavellian remarriage is a particularly intense form of flirtation; perhaps the endless task of "*learning* to speak the same language" is achieved through an agonistic, duel-like process very much like that of flirtation. Flirtation breaks down into a multiplicity of forms and formations of life, with various durations and scales. Marriage as presented by Cavell is an extreme case: flirtation extended in time, accented toward the pole of sameness and, it must be said, restricted to the heterosexual dyad.[21] The flirtations we pursue here go beyond the confines of the heterosexual dyad privileged by the discourse of marriage, tilting too toward the queer and the animal.

Published the year after *Pursuits of Happiness*, Niklas Luhmann's *Love as Passion* is in many regards the perfect complement to Cavell's now classic work on (re)marriage.[22] Luhmann provides a historical genealogy of love, marriage, and their interrelation that is largely lacking in Cavell. Two aspects of Luhmann's project are worthy of mention in this context: his theorization of the "code of love" as a "generalized symbolic medium of communication"[23] and his insistence on the constitutive place of literature in the history of this code. According to Luhmann, this "generalized symbolic medium of communication" emerges largely in response to an impossibility built into the structure of love, which he terms "the reflexivity of reciprocal desire."[24] The "code of love" is generated both through and as literature, providing a series of continually evolving, provisional, functional solutions to this impossible reciprocal reflexivity; in his words, "general symbolic media of communication are primarily semantic devices which enable essentially improbable communications nevertheless to be made successfully."[25] While Luhmann's framework enables very many keen analyses of the communicative binds and double binds of love, his theory is nonetheless limited by its ultimate orientation toward "communicative success." It is precisely this limitation that our book addresses. In turning toward flirtation, we turn too toward that in language which is *not* exhausted by the communicative function—which is to say, toward the rhetorical and the aesthetic, or indeed toward literature itself.[26] We must, however, also draw attention to a certain risk of romanticizing or idealizing flirtation, of positioning it in too sharp an opposition to seduction and thus imagining it as beyond relations of power. Several of our contributions are particularly attentive to this danger, seeing in flirtation either a renunciation of sensuous pleasure in keeping with a certain capitalist alienation and asceticism (Fleming) or a highly refined technique of political seduction that works precisely by pretending to turn away from the political (Campe).

SIX FLIRTATIONS

In keeping with the dialogue-like structure of flirtation, this anthology gathers six pairs of scholars, one to deliver an essay on the topic, one to respond freely: Paul Fleming and Daniel Hoffman-Schwartz;

Rüdiger Campe and Arne Höcker; Elisabeth Strowick and Lauren Shizuko Stone; Barbara Vinken and Christophe Koné; John Hamilton and Sage Anderson; Jacques Lezra and Barbara Natalie Nagel. The anthology is divided into three thematic sections, "Meta-Flirtations," "Flirtation with the World," "Flirtation and Transgression," each beginning with a short interlude by one of the editors.

Meta-Flirtations

The anthology begins with the interlude "Barely Covered Banter: Flirtation in *Double Indemnity*," devoted to Billy Wilder's classic noir film. Daniel Hoffman-Schwartz introduces different filmic techniques of flirtation that are embraced by highly erotic double entendres that run the risk of going over the speed limit. The following pairing of flirtations can be characterized as meta-flirtations. Paul Fleming's "Coquetry Without End" opens the dialogue of flirtations by offering a series of theses drawn from Simmel's classic essay, at once making explicit Simmel's borrowing from the philosophical tradition (Aristotle, Kant) and putting Simmel into dialogue with twentieth-century thinkers (Freud, Heidegger, Adorno, Barthes, and Luhmann). Fleming's paper addresses flirtation in Simmel as a *gestural* mode, to be distinguished from the explicit discursivity of love as discussed by Barthes or Luhmann. Hoffman-Schwartz's response, "The Double Sense of the 'With': Rethinking Relation after Simmel," first probes the ambiguous semantics of "flirting with" (*kokettieren mit*) and then pursues Simmel's reference to Plato's *Symposium,* posing the question, in light of Plato's famous linking of love and philosophy, of what the move from love to flirtation means for thought itself.

Moving back to the beginnings of literature (and maybe to the beginnings of flirtation), in "Rhetoric's Flirtation with Literature, from Gorgias to Aristotle: The Epideictic Genre" Rüdinger Campe describes the movement from rhetoric to poetry in Gorgias's *Encomium of Helen* as rhetoric's convergence or flirtation with literature. Elaborating on Campe's work, in "Playing with Yourself: On the Self-Reference of Flirtation," Arne Höcker contrasts the rhetorical proto-literature of the *Encomium* with the modernist de-rhetoricizing of the classical scene of seduction in Kafka's famous parable "The Silence of the Sirens."

Flirtation with the World

From *flirting with another* and *flirting with oneself* we proceed in the second section to *flirting with the world*. Lauren Shizuko Stone's interlude, "Staging Appeal, Performing Ambivalence," following Judith Butler's work on gender and citationality, works through the provocative suggestion that flirtation is the *drag* of seduction and thus an experience of "abandon" or even a certain "giddiness." In her reading of Thomas Mann's *Felix Krull*, Elisabeth Strowick suggests that "life is a flirtation": in the scene of writing, flirtation's aesthetics of perception operate as a foray, a productive self-staging and digression. She reads this as a kind of miming imitation, gesturing only back toward itself, just as Krull's filigreed pen strokes double back on themselves. Krull's life as flirtation can thus be understood not as a confidence trick but as "nothing. It was only charming." In "The 'Irreducibly Doubled Stroke': Flirtation, Felicity, and Sincerity," Stone responds by mobilizing Austin's idea of the impure performative and thus reads the production of the mimetic self as the suggestive force that results from an oscillation between description and performance; she further proposes the possibility that the flirtatious character is one who earnestly "never means it" but who nonetheless can tell us something about the nature of ordinary sincerity.

Barbara Vinken's "Frill and Flirtation: Femininity in the Public Space" reads flirtation politically, as a threat to republican virtue and a deconstruction of masculine subjectivity. Vinken tests different countries, cities, and times with respect to their flirt potential. Though she sees the present-day United States as "a lousy place to flirt . . . too Republican and too well Reformed, too Protestant, no irony please," she finds in the gentlemen of Bacongo, a subversive culture of the Congo, "the new women" who bring fashion back into flirtation and flirtation back into the city by strategies of cross-dressing, peacocking, and postcolonial mimicry. In his response to Vinken, Christophe Koné tries to rehabilitate the United States as a place to flirt, while admitting that whether you have fun in the flirtation or are made fun of depends on your wit: "I love your X!" In "Learning to Flirt with Don Juan," Koné focuses not so much on the powerful seducer Don Juan as on the Don Juan whose "seductive power is not quite yet in full swing but . . . his flirtation is on full display."

Flirtation and Transgression

"Three Terrors of Flirtation" is the title of Barbara Natalie Nagel's interlude, which opens our final section. Looking at a range of examples, from Henry James and Thomas Mann to a particularly terrifying "missed connection" posted on Craigslist, Nagel draws attention, poignantly and unexpectedly, to the agonies of flirtation: anxiety and uncertainty, endlessness, and—for the male flirt, the most terrifying of all—the specter of feminine sovereignty. The last two pairings explore the limits of flirtation, which seem to coincide with the limits of the human, specifically in the figures of the animal and death. In "The Luxury of Self-Destruction: Flirting with Mimesis with Roger Caillois," John Hamilton compares Freud's critique of flirtation as "vapid" and "inane" with Plato's concept of mimesis. Hamilton further theorizes a link between mimesis and death by considering Caillois's writing on mimicry as a practice of mimetic self-expenditure: We exhaust ourselves by becoming like something else; this in turn constitutes the basis for a new form of community based in a shared loss of subjective mastery. With "Wartime Love Affairs and Deathly Flirtation: Freud and Caillois on Identifying with Loss," Sage Anderson follows up on Hamilton's organizing references; Anderson interrogates the indirect relationship between flirtation and mimesis in Freud, Plato, and Bataille while simultaneously pursuing the alluring suggestion of an alternative aesthetics in the work of Caillois.

In "Bestiality: Mediation *More Ferarum*," Jacques Lezra discloses how in Wilhelm Jensen's *Gradiva* and Freud's reading of the novella lizards, canaries, and flies become instances of bestiality that enables flirtation. In Freud and Jensen desire always goes through "the mediating figure of the animal that desires and is desired, whose custom, habit, or culture it is to express its desire as beasts do, *more bestiarum*." In the face of this bestiality Nagel asks whether *Gradiva* is still a flirtatious, or rather an obscene piece of literature. Insisting on the unacknowledged flirtatiousness of Jensen's novella, "Doing It as the Beasts Did: Intertextuality as Flirtation in *Gradiva*" traces the sexy animals in Jensen's text back to other animal media of flirtation from Goethe's *Werther* and Sacher-Masoch's *Venus in Furs*.

META-FLIRTATIONS

BARELY COVERED BANTER: FLIRTATION IN *DOUBLE INDEMNITY*

Daniel Hoffman-Schwartz

Let's start with a classic scene of flirtation. The scene is from Billy Wilder's 1944 noir film *Double Indemnity*.[1] Wilder wrote the screenplay with Raymond Chandler, adapted from James Cain's novella of the previous year.[2] The shift of medium entailed a slight shift of genre as well: The laconic ways of hardboiled fiction yield ever so slightly to the garrulousness of the contemporary genres associated with the still relatively new medium of sound film—the screwball comedy or, more pointedly, the subgenre Stanley Cavell has famously christened the "comedy of remarriage."[3] In a remarkable series of analyses, Cavell ties sound film (the "talkie") to the representation of conversation and in turn ties conversation to marriage understood as a "form of life" or "mode of association."[4] According to Cavell, these films ask the question "What does a happy marriage *sound* like?"[5] Depicting the conversation of not yet, never quite lovers rather than the negotiation of "the ordinary" within the dailiness of marriage, a scene from *Double Indemnity* might be thought to ask instead "What does *flirtation* sound like?" In this chattering noir, flirtation stands right between crime and romance. The slight generic displacement allows

13

not so much a correction to Cavell as a supplement; as we will see, conversation, indeed language itself, comes to look (or sound) rather different when grasped from the perspective of flirtation instead of that of marriage.

The protagonist, Walter Neff, is an insurance salesman, making a routine stop at a client's home in hopes of persuading him to renew his lapsed auto insurance. Mr. Diedrichsen is not home, but just before the maid can succeed in turning Neff away, *Mrs.* Diedrichsen (Phyllis) verbally intervenes from off-screen. The camera first gives us the gazes of Neff and the maid looking toward the unseen figure before quickly switching to a point-of-view shot looking up at Phyllis, who has appeared on the upstairs landing, clad in nothing but a towel (see Figure 1). Unperturbed by the distance or her own state of relative undress, Phyllis rather boldly takes over the conversation. As Neff explains the situation, the conversation stumbles, tellingly, on the word *risk*: "How do you do, Mrs. Diedrichsen? I'm Walter Neff, Pacific Oil Risk." "Pacific Oil what?" "Pacific Oil Risk Insurance Company." *Risk* here is a metonymic elision of "risk *insurance*." The implied presence of the elided term, however, makes all the difference, distinguishing the attempted negation of risk from risk itself. The emphatically performed nonhearing ("Pacific Oil what?") betrays a deliberate incomprehension of the elision, which points back to the unconscious motivation for such an elision in the first place: *risk* is far more alluring than *risk insurance*.

In drawing attention to what Neff has actually said rather than what he has implied, Phyllis alerts us to a libidinal investment in risk itself, a libidinal investment that would seem to shadow any attempt to manage, minimize, or anticipate risk. In flirting, the bored insurance man, the would-be master of chance, finally gets to experience the risk that he must relentlessly conjure and exorcise in his work.[6] To wit, Georg Simmel, in his classic analysis of flirtation, writes of a "pleasure in chance" or indeed a "*hazardous* pleasure" ("Lust am Hazard").[7] Simmel goes on to argue that this risk is "arrested and stabilized" in flirtation, as in the manner of a mere game without any real

FIGURE 1

stakes, but he stipulates as well that *some* reference to actual effects (*Wirklichkeit*) *must* be present in flirtation.[8] Flirtation is structured by the possibility of the transgression of its own form and formality; flirtation would not be itself if it did not hold out the possibility, however distantly, of going beyond mere flirtation. *Double Indemnity* presents the extreme instance: flirtation consummated not in sex but in death, the eventual murder of Mr. Diedrichsen committed jointly by Neff and Phyllis.[9] The stakes are high indeed, inasmuch as Phyllis and Neff have wagered their very freedom on the success or failure of their plot. Death figures sex, but it also comes to replace sex as the figure for reality;[10] the series of metaphoric substitutions points to the problematic character of the reality projected by flirtation as its structuring limit. In the double temporality of the film, with its apparent present tense unfolding also as Neff's recollection and confession, the movement from the irreal, game-like quality of a flirtation that merely thematizes risk to the risk-laden consummation both is and is not necessary. We watch the flirtation as a "pure" flirtation—purposive without purpose, unbound from teleology—*and* we watch it as the fateful moment within which the unfolding of future events is already preinscribed.[11]

After this initial evocation of risk, the flirtation begins in earnest (or not so earnest). Neff's explanation of the situation all but immediately settles on a double entendre: "The insurance ran out on the fifteenth. I'd hate to think of your having a smashed fender or something while you're not . . . fully covered." Neff delivers the line with a slight hesitation and a hard swallow, as if he is unsure whether the remark he is about to make constitutes a lapsus or a witticism. The double entendre erotically diverts the metaphor of coverage from the domain of insurance, troping the term precisely by reliteralizing it. The erotic is itself double here: It is one semantic field among others— that of, for instance, the body, covered or otherwise. But it is also the movement between fields—not merely the displaying and hiding of a particular body but the displaying and hiding of the fact that we are talking about bodies at all. Put slightly differently, *coverage* is a figure for figuration itself, a self-thematizing figure. Besides this properly figurative register, the line is inflected with an irony akin to that of psychoanalytic negation, wish barely disguised as fear: "I'd hate to think of it." One might say that Neff's language, like Phyllis's body, is itself barely covered.

After the brief interval required for Phyllis to dress herself, she and Neff reconvene in the living room. She strides confidently and decisively to a mirror, checking her hair and putting on lipstick, her movements accompanied by the sardonic announcement "I hope I've got my face on straight," the oblique angle of the camera wryly reframing her lines. The mirror enables a spatial configuration that constitutes something like a classical diagram for flirtation as such: Phyllis stands with her back to Neff as she examines herself in the mirror, his reflection therefore in the background of her own; she is, in other words, simultaneously turned toward him and turned away from him, self-examination coinciding with self-display (see Figure 2).[12]

FIGURE 2.

This act of specular self-absorption performed for the other produces a curious intimacy; it is as if the living room has been transformed, fleetingly at least, into a boudoir. The avowal of artifice is itself carefully, artfully staged. Her witticism ("I hope I've got my face on straight") to some degree simply repeats this avowal, translating gestural flirtation into its verbal equivalent. But it adds one further abyssal tropological turn: Not only does she avow that her face is masked (troped, figured), but the avowal is itself figurative in the most disturbing way, with the would-be literality of the face coming to figure the mask.[13]

The conversation passes from her face to his name: "Neff's the name, isn't it?" The newly emboldened Neff launches a rather aggressively disorienting volley back at Phyllis: "With two F's, like in Philadelphia, if you know the story." The roles again reversed, Phyllis, now "fully covered" but somehow also less defended, this time does not play along in the game of codes but instead asks a naked question that exposes her lack of mastery: "What story?" Neff's reply: "*The*

Philadelphia Story." There is more at stake in Neff's spelling lesson than feigned stupidity. The reference to a fictional text as such thematizes the scene's artificiality and game-like play-acting.[14] But it is not just any fictional text to which Neff refers; it is rather one of Cavell's paradigmatic "comedies of remarriage." We are again close to a lapsus: Perhaps Neff flirts with sincerity here, imagining himself giving up his dissolute bachelor ways for the love of a good woman, as Cary Grant's Dexter Haven ultimately does for Katharine Hepburn's Tracy Lord in the film version of *The Philadelphia Story*.[15] "Neff," the monosyllabic name suitable for a hard-boiled hero, mingles absurdly with the pseudo-classical "Philadelphia," with its associations of brotherly love or *philia*.[16] And yet if we take Cavell's emphasis on sound literally—more literally than does Cavell himself—Neff's joke begins to make a different kind of sense: In the world of banter, organized by the *auditory* materiality of the signifier, "Philadelphia" *does* in a way have two F's, like "Neff." The fantasy of sincerity dissolves into the excess of sonorous materiality, an excess that haunts Cavell's chattering "talkies" from within. Sound *as* sound, the materiality of spoken language, irreducibly aesthetic, belongs more to the conversational domain of flirtation than to that of marriage.

THE ART OF FLIRTATION: SIMMEL'S COQUETRY WITHOUT END

Paul Fleming

Sigmund Freud did not hold flirtation in high regard. In his 1915 essay "Thoughts for the Times on War and Death," Freud compares "an American flirtation [*ein amerikanischer Flirt*]" to "a continental love-affair [*kontinentale Liebesbeziehung*],"[1] and it doesn't require a deep knowledge of psychoanalysis to guess on which side of the opposition he lands, and not simply because the deck is stacked by being cast in terms of his well-known distaste for the United States. There is, however, much at stake in this juxtaposition, for the simple reason that Freud locates the difference between flirtation and a love affair precisely in the stakes involved: In flirtation "it is understood from the first that nothing is to happen," while in a love affair "both partners must constantly bear its serious consequences in mind."[2] It is somewhat surprising that, writing six months after the outbreak of the Great War, Freud would turn to flirtation to open the essay's second section, "Our Relation to Death," but for Freud life, and thus erotic life, acquires meaning only when something is at stake, which his notion of flirtation utterly lacks: "Life becomes impoverished, it loses its interest, if the highest wager in the game of life [*der höchste*

Einsatz in den Lebensspielen], life itself, may not be risked."[3] Richness and interest are pegged to the possibility of loss, especially the ulti-mate one: death. Quite literally one needs to ante up in the game of life to bestow it with import, and flirtation for Freud risks nothing, expects nothing, and thus has nothing to win or to lose. Freud can argue thus because he views the difference between flirtation and a love affair as merely one of degree, not kind; coquetry is simply an impoverished version of much richer—because riskier—erotic games.

Georg Simmel's pair of early twentieth-century essays, "Flirtation" (1909/1923, "Die Koketterie") and "The Sociology of Sociability" (1910/1911, "Die Soziologie der Geselligkeit") offers a counterargu-ment to Freud's ascertaining a lack of seriousness in flirtation. If Freud views flirtation as a diminished version of a love affair, Simmel places it in a different order or sociological field, what he calls "sociability" (*Geselligkeit*),[4] and thus circumvents the brunt of Freud's argument concerning impoverishment.[5] Sociability is *"play-form of association* and is related to the content-determined concreteness of association as art is related to reality."[6] Simmel's crucial analogy therefore runs thus: Flirtation is to an affair what art is to reality. Insofar as coquet-ry's form is derived from life (e.g., the erotics of seduction, courtship, an affair) and raised to the level of a game, of play with no goal be-yond itself, then "coquetry plays out the forms of eroticism."[7] On the one hand, Simmel agrees with Freud that, yes, nothing is to happen in flirtation, but on the other, he makes the claim that this is not co-quetry's poverty but its plentitude.

This essay does not attempt to elaborate the entire richness of Sim-mel's thoughts on flirtation or coquetry (terms I will use interchange-ably),[8] especially when it comes to gender relations around 1900, a task that would exceed the limits of this localized intervention into the phenomenon of flirtation.[9] Rather, in the spirit of the present vol-ume, this set of theses hopes to circumscribe elements of the dis-cursive field delimiting flirtation—as a practice, a form, and a mode of relating. One of the guiding premises is that the relatively undertheorized terrain of flirtation is too often understood in terms of seduction. It is admittedly difficult to hold flirtation and seduction strictly apart—conceptually, practically—but there is nevertheless a difference (a gliding and perhaps ultimately trangressable difference) that these theses try to underscore, which is precisely what drives Simmel's thoughts and gives them their urgency.[10] What follows are six theses that draw extensively from and play on Simmel's attempt to situate flirtation this side (the playful, artistic, sociable side) of seduction, followed by a caveat from the other side.

THESIS 1: SEDUCTION MAY BE AN ART, BUT ONLY FLIRTATION IS ART

Seduction wants something; it desires some *thing*—to have, to possess the other. Seduction has a vested interest, a *telos*, an end. Therefore, while one often speaks of the "art of seduction," it is *an* art in the sense of *techne*—a purposeful art, a set of skills, whose aim is clear. Its means may be many; its goal, however, is strictly delimited. Flirtation, following Simmel, is different. Simmel was in many ways a neo-Kantian, especially when it came to art and play.[11] In what is thus a rather strict Kantian sense, flirtation approximates the status of fine art. In his essay on sociability, Simmel declares that one can "speak with some right of the 'art'—not only the 'arts'—of coquetry" (" *'Kunst'—nicht nur von den 'Künsten'—der Koketterie*").[12]

Coquetry achieves the status of art by fulfilling two central modalities of Kant's judgment of the beautiful: First, flirtation is defined by disinterested pleasure ("*Wohlgefallen ohne alles Interesse*"). Unlike seduction, flirtation is not about the object, its existence or possession. In both art and flirtation one finds a certain indifference to the existence of the object.[13] To flirt in order to win over and thus "have" the other in whatever sense is to move into seduction; it is the shift from the strictly aesthetic domain to the world of empirical desire, from Kant's beautiful to his "merely agreeable," which may best describe the quasi-art of seduction. Seduction is not content merely to contemplate but takes an active, lively interest in the real existence of the object of desire. "Hence one says of the agreeable," writes Kant, "not merely that it pleases but that it gratifies. It is not mere approval that I give, rather inclination is thereby aroused."[14] Flirtation, in contrast, is pleasure that does not aspire to gratification; it is pleasurable approval without (seduction's) aroused inclination.

Second, and perhaps more important, Simmel maintains that Kant's essential designation of the judgment of the beautiful as "purposiveness without purpose" "holds true for flirtation to the greatest extent possible."[15] Appearing *as if* it had a further goal or purpose, flirtation in fact remains self-contained, not going beyond itself. To put it bluntly, in true mutual flirtation (as opposed to seduction, courtship, or the like) the goal is not to sleep with the other. Flirtation is not a means to an end. Rather, as a form of sociability, flirtation "in its pure form has no ulterior end, no content, and no result outside of itself."[16] The nonpurposive logic of flirtation is thus somewhat tautological: One flirts with someone *in order to* flirt with someone and thus enjoy the pleasing effect of this free, disinterested play. Coquetry is an end-in-itself and thus without end.

THESIS 2: LOVE HAS ITS DISCOURSE; FLIRTATION HAS ITS GESTURES

As Roland Barthes and Niklas Luhmann have demonstrated in elaborate and loving detail, love has a language, a semantic field that has been continually worked out, modified, and codified over the centuries of the modern subject, particularly as the lover's discourse differentiates itself from friendship, family relations, and so on.[17] Perhaps trite—but therefore all the more secure and clear—the established lexicon of love circumscribes what the lover can and cannot, should and should not say. Thus it is no surprise that love has developed an entire industry of cards, poems, plays, and presents; the words of love are quotable, iterable, immediately recognizable. One cannot say the same about flirtation, which is less lexical (it is not a semantic field) and more gestural. In other words, flirtation is less about language, about saying, and is more concerned with gestures as a particular form of *actio in distans*. The quintessential gesture of flirtation is the view askance, always at a remove, ideally from across the room. If the lover looks deep into the beloved's eyes, holding and fixing the gaze, the flirtatious glance is half turned away, its object uncertain, its duration often the blink of an eye. Even if such a sideways glance counts among flirtation's "more banal guise[s]," such a gesture already contains coquetry's entire force of simultaneous "consent and refusal," in which the gaze's withdrawal is "prefigured" in the very moment of its being cast.[18]

This gestural mixture of simultaneously turning toward and away can be described as apostrophic. Like a poetic-linguistic apostrophe ("O, you with whom I flirt"), the one flirting gestures toward, addresses the other by turning away; he or she calls out to the other person by remaining silent. The one who flirts acts, but only at a distance. Flirtation is thus neither the traditional "love at first sight" nor Baudelaire's famous modern "love at last sight." Rather, because it is not love at all, because it is nonteleological in its intentions, flirtation adheres to the exemplary logic of the German *Bei-spiel*[19] (example), literally "a playing alongside": The rhetoric of flirtation's gestures circumscribe a field of play—always at a distance—alongside the other person, alongside desire, alongside interest.[20] For this reason Simmel quite brilliantly notes that flirtation "loves to busy itself with peripheral things: with dogs or flowers or children."[21] This fundamental gesture of flirtation, this *bei-spielhafte* form of apostrophe, says "I turn away from you, and turn toward this dog, this flower, this child, and in so doing show how good I am at playfully immersing myself in things—one of which isn't you. And yet I play all this in front of you, for you, so you see what you are missing—and Fido is getting."[22] Of course, flirtation says none of that; it just plays with the dog, and this gesture says it all. This "saying it all" takes place, however, in a nonverbal gesture that possesses, in Richard Kaye's words, the flirtatious advantage of leaving "no solid traces and thus no incriminating 'evidence.' "[23] In this paraplay, in the pleasure of the para-, it would nevertheless be a mistake to declare the dog an *Ersatz* for the other; in flirtation there is no possible substitution, for example, exchanging the dog for the one with whom you are flirting. The dog is essential to the gestural constellation of flirtation, a triangle of movement in which one acts, plays, enjoys only at a distance. If one were to give a name to the gestural rhetorics of flirtation, one could call it *Bei-Spielen*.

THESIS 3: FLIRTATION OFFERS A UNIQUE MODE OF *MITSEIN*

Flirtation enacts a multiplied mode of *Mitsein*, of being-with, because it doubles the sense of "co" or "with." As I already hinted with *actio in distans*, the one flirting plays with the other person as both an instrument *and* as a partner, an object *and* a playmate.[24] The premise of flirtation, at least as Simmel imagines it in its full form, implies a contract: "We are both (just) flirting here." This point is essential. Just as S&M has its clear rules, agreements, and code words, flirtation requires an unspoken agreement, a silent pact of mutual understanding. If all involved have not implicitly agreed to the game of flirtation, if one person is "merely a victim who is involuntarily carried along,"[25] then for Simmel one cannot speak of coquetry in all its sociable (playful, artful) fullness; rather it possesses a potentially sadistic side, the expression of power or manipulation. In its pure form, that is, as form without further purpose, flirtation demands that it be play "among *equals*"[26] and thus divorced of means-ends instrumentality.[27] In other words, in the unspoken agreement constituting the full sociable flirt, one freely enters into a game and thus is not *really* an instrument, is not a "pawn in the game" but merely plays one—consciously, willfully, with pleasure.[28]

To flirt in its full form, in which all people knowingly flirt, is to mutually enjoy the *Bei-Spiel*, the *Mit-Spiel*, the "playing with"—the playing alongside *as* playing with. We play together, with each other, by playing apart, showering and withholding attention, by giving our caresses to Fido, our attention to the flowers, our laughs to our other friends. Like Hegel's notion of parabasis in comedy from the *Phenomenology of Spirit*, it is playing with the mask in the dual sense of wearing a mask (*maskiert spielen*) and to have the mask in the hand, to have dropped it, and now to play with it as a prop.[29] One could thus venture the thesis that coquetry is thus closer to comedy than to tragedy (which has a special relation to love), but with the difference that coquetry doesn't end with marriage, as comedy so often does. Coquetry is comedy without end, comedy without an end.

THESIS 4: FLIRTATION IS AN ADVANCED VERSION OF *FORT-DA*

As a well-orchestrated coordination of give and take, of dropping and raising the mask, of offering and withdrawing, flirtation is a continuation of the child's pleasure found in Freud's *fort-da*. Whereas the child repeats in the mode of play the dynamics of disappearance and return, and thus pleasurably masters loss, flirtation could be called *fort-da* for advanced students of pleasure, since loss and its mastery are no longer at stake.[30] Unlike *fort-da* for beginners, the joy resides not merely in the *da,* in the reappearance of the desired object, but also and especially in the *fort* as a mode of being *da,* a presence that appears only at a distance, in absence. The logic of flirtation is not simply to hide or conceal or withdraw. That is not flirtation but shyness, insecurity, or a lack of self-confidence. Rather, like a fig leaf, flirtation hides in order to draw attention. This structural aspect is central because it also explains the erotics of flirtation. Referring to ethnography, Simmel explicitly connects flirtation to the erotics of concealment. The covering of one's genitalia originally had nothing to do with shame; "rather, it served only the need for ornamentation and the closely related intention of exercising sexual attraction by means of concealment."[31] The one flirting comes into the open by concealing

himself or herself. Flirtation is a permanent play of synchronic presence and absence, for the one flirting is never "there" for the taking.
And that is the allure. In flirtation one withdraws in order to gain
attention, to stand out by standing aside. In other words, to be a coquette is to offer oneself in the mode and movement of withdrawal.
One makes oneself *fort* in order to be *da*. It is a simultaneous yes and
no,[32] which is not to be confused with the violent logic of "no means
yes" or the dream logic that knows no no. Rather one announces
one's desire by concealing it—which is not the same as having no desire; instead desire is held forth, presented in its concealedness.

THESIS 5: FLIRTATION IS PERMANENT EXTRADECISIONISM

If the sovereign for Carl Schmitt is the one who decides the exception,[33] flirtation is the exception in which nothing is to be decided.
If flirtation concerns power, then it is the power that lies in the state
or moment *exterior* to decision. To be clear: Flirtation is not the moment *before* decision, nor is it a case of undecidability (e.g., "Should
I stay or should I go?"; "Do I want/not want?"; "Do I have a chance or
not?"). Rather flirtation is the decision to *not* participate in the world
of decision, since as nonteleological, playful *Mitsein*, there is nothing to decide. In flirtation one crucial decision is made: the decision
to flirt, and thus to make no further decisions, since "every conclu-
sive decision brings flirtation to an end."[34] Flirtation thereby constitutes the power of not deciding, where a lack of decisiveness, of decision becomes pleasure itself. Flirtation can thus be counted among
Herbert Marcuse's negative freedoms: the freedom *from* choice, to
remove oneself from the economy of exchange.[35]

THESIS 6: FLIRTATION IS OUT OF TIME

Because flirtation is not about seducing, winning, gaining, or having the other but rather the pure play of desire without end, it adheres to no temporality of futurity. Utterly in the moment, the one

flirting does not ask "What comes next?" because for the flirt there is no "next" step, just now-time, the time of flirtation. As pure presence flirtation is a mode, an act of "no future," since its time is the time of *pure provisionality*. Therefore, while flirtation is often described under the temporality of deferral, this is the case only if one views it as of a piece, on a continuum with seduction; coquetry would be just "putting off the inevitable" as opposed to a game and pleasure in its own right. When Kaye thus cites the quintessential coquettish gesture of *always* putting off the next dance (as described in the 1851 treatise *The Natural History of the Flirt*), this gesture can be called "deferral" only in the sense that deferral becomes permanent and thus defers nothing. It is a permanent state of waiting without expectation for anything to come or happen.

Therefore, in flirtation the provisional is the ultimate, final form of temporality—provisionality without end, a provisionality "not conditioned by something final."[36] Flirtation can thus be described not as the *promesse de bonheur* but only *as a pure promise*: the happiness that there is a promise at all, a promise that promises nothing. One could thus reverse Theodor Adorno's famous formula about art and describe flirtation as the *bonheur de promesse*, the pleasure of the promise itself, because it has no end beyond itself and thus time folds back onto itself as the moment.[37] "The promise of happiness," Simmel writes in regard to coquetry, "already anticipates a part of the happiness attained."[38] Therefore, since it is not predicated on possessing or having, flirtation never walks away empty-handed; flirtation comprises "having" in the mode of not having, of not having to have.

CAVEAT, INSTEAD OF A CONCLUSION

Susan Laxton provides a perfect summary of Simmel's ideal notion of flirtation: "Simmelian play forms are pure active experience exempt from exchange value: they play themselves out and then everyone goes home."[39] This is exactly what is to happen when flirtation

is carefully distinguished from seduction—except that sometimes
things play themselves out differently, and everyone goes home together.

One senses the potential for flirtation gliding into seduction in the
degree to which Simmel strives to delimit it as pure play. At flirtation's
heights, when both people consent to the "free moving play," the
erotic lurks not as a possibility but solely as "a remote symbol"; at
this juncture coquetry "has left behind the reality of erotic desire, of
consent or denial, and becomes a reciprocal play of shadow pictures
[*Wechselspiele der Silhouetten*] of these serious matters."[40] This metaphor of shadow play runs throughout Simmel's discussions of forms
of sociability and is telling precisely in its negation of a body—and
thus of "real" or "serious" erotic desire, which it "has left behind."
Simmel's notion of flirtation thereby transposes life "into the symbolic game of its shadow-realm, in which there is no friction, because
shadows cannot bump into each other."[41] This metaphoric field of non-
corporeality would seem to safeguard flirtation from falling prey to
the fate of Dante's Paolo and Francesca, whose innocent reading of
Lancelot's pure *amor* culminates in the famous scene of seduction
and closing of the book: "We read no further that day."[42] If coquetry
is only a play of shadows, never shall two bodies meet.

Although Simmel consistently aligns coquetry with aesthetic categories such as disinterested pleasure, purposiveness without purpose, and the pure play of forms, he nevertheless admits one crucial
difference between art and flirtation: "Unlike the artist, however, they
[flirters] do not play with the appearance of reality but rather with
reality itself."[43] This inextricable relation to reality opens the possibility that reality in turn plays with the flirters, beckons them, tempts
them to have a body in all senses. Therefore a structural feature con-
ditioning the pleasure of flirtation comes from flirting with reality and
thus risking to put an end to the game. Flirtation, in other words, always flirts with the real and thus with seduction. This *is* the game, the
art of flirtation: to flirt with seduction, to touch upon its border, and
still refrain from crossing over. In fact such temptation is inherent

in the structure of "semi-concealment"[44] that Simmel diagnoses as the essential gesture of simultaneous withdrawal and drawing attention. Concealing so as to attract produces (if only in imagination) what one could call a superwhole, a hypertotality, since concealment engenders a fullness that only fantasy can fulfill: "The whole is fantasized all the more urgently [*eindringlicher*], and the desire for the totality of reality is excited all the more consciously and intensively."[45] Precisely by *playing with reality* flirtation inflames fantasy (and desire) the most. Even within the gendered parameters of Simmel's exploration of flirtation, one has to reverse Adorno's infamous dictum: When it comes to coquetry, it is the women with the *most* fantasy, who inflame fantasy the most.[46]

There is thus nothing inherent in flirtation to prevent it from becoming seduction; on the contrary, it must always play with its possibility. More important, there is no reason to preclude the possibility of any relationship from moving back and forth between modes and moments of flirtation and seduction. By reading Simmel's "Flirtation" and Ovid's *Ars amatoria* together, Timothy Perper opens up the possibility of flirtation accompanying all modes of erotic life: "For Simmel, it is thus possible to flirt at each of the Ovidian stages, most intensely perhaps, during naked sexual involvement itself. Then each orgasm hints flirtatiously that another exists *in potential*, and it is the *possibility* that is alluring."[47] Here both Simmel and Freud receive a small comeuppance; inherent in every flirt is the possibility of seduction, just as every seduction, as part of its excitement and inexhaustibility, demands an aspect of flirtation, of what may be pure play.

One could end here, but one has to add another critical addendum to the six theses, a further critical possibility or perspective, that may be an inversion: *Maybe this is all wrong.* Maybe flirtation is not art, not an elevated feeling, not pure provisionality and freedom from exchange. Or it is all of this and therefore within a libidinal economy (since we are, if only on a structural level, talking about libido, about eros in all its forms) it is nothing to be celebrated, nothing to be desired but rather another form of what Adorno famously calls "castrated hedonism," his description of Kantian aesthetics as "desire without desire."[48]

From this perspective flirtation would be the pleasure of renouncing or withholding pleasure. Its lack of interest is indeed its lack, its refusal to seek further, other pleasure. As pleasure without interest and purposiveness without purpose, perhaps flirtation is ultimately a form of joy without *jouissance*. And here too flirtation has its relation to art, art in the mode of compartmentalization and renunciation, drawn from the dawn of the West: the song of the Sirens and Odysseus strapped to the mast. From this perspective Odysseus would also offer the archetype of flirtation, of pleasure at a distance, of the pleasure of mere contemplation, of the need to look away while being drawn toward.

The Sirens however are seducers; they are not in on the game of paraplaying, of playing alongside and thus with Odysseus. They want him to want them, and he of course wants them, to have them or be had by them. The cunning Odysseus, however, surrenders himself to pleasure by having himself bound to the mast; the more beautiful the singing, the tighter the ropes. Odysseus is thus also the great resister, *the one who converts seduction to flirtation*. Odysseus, the master, masters himself and thus only flirts with disaster, which equally means flirting with fulfillment. He flirts with seduction and wins, neutralizing the allure of the Sirens and turning their song of seduction into fine art, into an object of pleasurable contemplation. The Sirens become mere art, divorced from practice, while Odysseus learns the pleasure of not having to decide, of having no decision, of being beyond decision. Tied to the mast, he learns the pleasure of pure play. Like all true flirters—and I conclude with this phrase in all its ambivalence—Odysseus gets it all by getting nothing.

"THE DOUBLE-SENSE OF THE 'WITH' ": RETHINKING RELATION AFTER SIMMEL

Daniel Hoffman-Schwartz

This response essay is in two parts: first, a close engagement with a single one of Paul Fleming's six theses on flirtation and its textual basis in Simmel's "On Flirtation"; and second, a caveat of my own. The first part tries to elaborate the problematic of relation (or "withness") that Fleming opens in Simmel; the caveat attempts to account for the specific exemplarity of flirtation as a topos for theory.

Thesis 3 is "Flirtation offers a unique mode of *Mitsein*." To phrase it this way is to evoke Heidegger or Jean-Luc Nancy, the thinker who has most rigorously pursued Heidegger's concept of *Mitsein*.[1] In passing I should note that this is indicative of Fleming's general strategy for reading Simmel; Simmel's deceptively casual, inventive, yet precise relation to the German philosophical tradition grants his texts a peculiar latency that lends itself in turn to the sort of theoretical amplification and cross-referencing practiced by Fleming. Following Fleming's post-Heideggerian reformulation of Simmel, one might say that flirtation is a play with the "with," a way of thematizing, negotiating, and perhaps even working through the originary sociality or exposure to others that *is* being-in-the-world. There is a kind of leap involved in such a reading: We spring from the sociology of modernity to fundamental ontology. If Mitsein (Being-with) is "unique," to cite Fleming's terms, it leads us to *Dasein* (Being-there) and ultimately *Sein* (Being). In flirtation we would thus obscurely attempt to apprehend a "being-with" that eludes us precisely for being fundamental. I will show to what extent such a reflection on an ontological "withness" lurks within Simmel's ostensibly sociological reflections.

Simmel, it is important to note, does not write directly about the "with" as such. Beginning at the level of everyday (German) language, he takes his cue instead from the curious semantics of the expression "to flirt with" (*kokettieren mit*). This makes a certain kind of sense: As pure relation, the "with" can be accessed only indirectly. Following Simmel, "to flirt with" (*kokettieren mit*) is an ambiguous syntagm that suggests two seemingly mutually exclusive possibilities: On one hand, there is a collaborative, symmetrical "flirting with," in relation to which Simmel can write of the figure of the "partner";[2] on the other hand, there is also an instrumental sense of "flirting with," which renders the would-be partner a mere tool. This semantic ambiguity characterizes the use of the "with" in general; for instance, one plays tennis "with a partner" but also "with a racket and ball." This ambiguity, Simmel seems to suggest, is reflected and intensified in the specificity of "*flirting* with," as though it offers the proper form or mode within which to apprehend this curious ambiguity of the "with."

The emphasis on instrumentality is rather scandalous. Simmel seems to suggest that the possibility of being instrumentalized by the other is an intrinsic aspect of flirtation, even an intrinsic aspect of the *pleasure* of flirtation; if one could somehow guarantee or prove that the flirt were "in good faith," it would not be flirtation at all.[3] In flirtation good faith is bad faith, or so it would seem. The Kantian subject for whom every other subject is an end in itself rather than a means would thus have to forbid itself the pleasures of flirtation. Whether this would speak against flirtation or against the *Metaphysics of Morals* is an open question.[4] As if disturbed by his own insight,

Simmel seems at times to transform this double meaning into a new, third sense that is the sublation (*Aufhebung*) of the other two: from the seemingly mutually exclusive possibilities of "flirting with" as instrumentalization and "flirting with" as collaboration follows the appearance of something like reciprocal instrumentalization, a partnership between human tools or tool-humans.

It is perhaps instructive to take a closer look at the particularly complex if not altogether convoluted passage in which the "double-sense of the 'with'" ("Doppelbedeutung des <mit>") is introduced. Here relation turns into a kind of math problem: The figure of the "double-sense of the 'with'" emerges in the discussion of a scene that is not reciprocal and reversible but is in fact triangular. The scene is characterized by the presence, virtual or actual, of a third, a spectator *for whom* one flirts—that is, in fact, a spectator *with whom* one flirts by seeming to flirt with another, more proximate other. Let's look at Simmel's long formulation; note the turn from an illusory two that is in fact a three back to a seemingly closed dyadic reciprocity; note too a further twist, namely that this reciprocity is suspended in the subjunctive; note finally as well the manner in which the whole passage is cast as a kind of revelation or disclosure (*Offenbarung*) of the "deep sense" of "with," thus leading in an ontological direction: "When a woman flirts 'with' one man in order to flirt with another who is the actual object of her intentions [*auf den es in Wirklichkeit abgesehen ist*], the double-meaning of the word 'with' is profoundly revealed [*offenbart sich der eigentümliche Tiefsinn, der in der Doppelbedeutung des <mit> liegt*]"; this is followed by the unremarked transition from an actual three to a subjunctive two: "On the one hand, it refers to an instrument, on the other hand, to the member of a correlation, *as if* we [*als könne man*] could not make a person into a mere means [*bloße(s) Mittel*] without this functioning in a reciprocal and retroactive fashion as well [*ohne daß dies zugleich Rückwirkung und Wechselbeziehung zugleich wäre*]."[5] It is *as if* there is a reciprocal relation or a retroactive effect. But this can never be assured, not least of all because the entire specular interaction between

Flirts One and Two may itself be a specular show for Flirt Three. It is thus not so much a matter of two becoming three as a matter of n+1 flirts; the uncertain line between the spectator *in* the tableau of flirtation and the spectator *of* the tableau of flirtation is in fact part of what is at stake in flirtation itself. We never know who really is watching us flirt or who is virtually flirting with another by watching us *being flirted with*; flirtation merges with surveillance. Our own technological epoch only radicalizes the possibilities of flirtation as *actio in distans* named by Fleming; flirtation was always already tele-flirtation.

There is yet another complication in the passage, bearing on the problem of sexual difference. As I noted earlier, the reciprocity is cast in the subjunctive. The problematic character of this reciprocity stems in part from the stubborn *irreversibility* of what is implicitly Simmel's paradigmatic utterance for the double sense: "The woman flirts with a man" ("Die Frau kokettiert mit einem Mann"). According to the terms of Simmel's essay, the inverse sentence, "The man flirts with a woman" ("Der Mann kokettiert mit einer Frau"), seems to be some-thing like an impossible utterance, thus radically short-circuiting the promise of reciprocity tied to the sublation of the two senses of "flirt-ing with."[6] In other words, a man can *be flirted with* in the double sense of *being instrumentalized* and being a partner, but, according to Simmel's speculative semantics, he can *flirt with* only in the single sense of being a partner. For if a man too actively flirts, he risks be-coming a coquet, in German *eine Kokette* in the feminine; Simmel's hesitation thus corresponds to a kind of embedded but unthematized queer moment in his argument.[7] The essay drives toward reciprocity and symmetry precisely as a resistance to its own scandalous implica-tion of a pleasure in instrumentality, but the insistence on symmetry and reciprocity pushes the essay to the verge of a further scandal that it cannot quite name: the scandal of the male coquet.

In closing, my own caveat: Simmel's text begins with what he calls "Plato's wisdom concerning love"; love is, in Simmel's paraphrase, "a middle state [*ein mittlerer Zustand*] between having and not-having."[8]

It is this mediating or intermediary character that ties together love and philosophy in the *Symposium*. Philosophy and eros are both structured by a lack and therefore a capacity to desire, a capacity lacking in the gods; philosophy and eros are both, in other words, paradoxical privileges of finitude. Quoting Diotima's speech: "In fact, you see, none of the gods loves wisdom or wants to become wise—for they are wise—and no one else who is wise already loves wisdom; on the other hand, no one who is ignorant will love wisdom either or want to become wise."[9] And then a bit later on: "It follows that Love [*Eros*]"—here mythically embodied—"*must* be a lover of wisdom and, as such, is in between being wise and being ignorant."[10] Though Simmel does not thematize the self-reflective character of the philosophical inquiry into love, it inevitably hovers in the background after this Platonic opening gambit. It leads to the question of the *exemplarity* of flirtation for Simmel's own philosophical or theoretical project.

According to Simmel, flirtation, distinct from love as defined by Plato's Diotima, makes having and not-having simultaneous; completing the analogy with the *Symposium*, flirtation would make superfluous the *desire* whose intellectual form is *speculation*.[11] Where there is flirtation, so goes this line of thought, there can be no speculative philosophy. Going back to where my essay began, I am thus posing the question of how best to understand finitude. The *Symposium* itself is hardly decided on this matter: On one side, it is desire that propels the ("Platonic") movement from finitude to the Idea, desire itself transformed (or sublimated) in the process; on the other side, desire remains lack, tied to the ironic ("Socratic") disposition, famously captured in the formula "I know that I don't know."[12] Indeed this very coexistence in the *Symposium* of mutually contradictory understandings of love comes itself to figure something very much like Being-with. Though Simmel seems eager at times to distance himself from flirtation—he too does not want to be perceived as a flirt (*eine Kokette*)—there does seem to be something flirtatious about his way of proceeding. On a formal level one might note Simmel's penchant for italics, the typographic equivalent of the sidelong glance he mentions elsewhere in the essay. His formulations even exchange such typographic glances: "the art of *pleasing*" alternates with the "*art* of pleasing"; "*play* with reality" flirts with "play with *reality*."[13] On the level of method it is worth citing Simmel's lines from the preface to *Philosophische Kultur,* the volume in which "On Flirtation" originally appeared:

> In so far as philosophical assertions diverge so much that they cannot be united and not one of them possesses uncontested validity, but since one nonetheless senses something common among them, the value of which survives any criticism of the individual element and carries the philosophical process further and further onwards, then that which they have in common cannot lie in any particular content but in the process itself. This may of course be obvious as a reason for leaving the name philosophy unscathed.[14]

Here Simmel's emphasis on "the *name* philosophy" deliberately recalls the *philia* in philosophy, which is repressed in the flirtation essay's treatment of the *Symposium* as a text merely about love; taking a cue from what now appears to be the flirtatious "being-with" of the *Symposium* itself, we can perhaps read in Simmel's essay a tacit reinterpretation of the *philia* in philosophy. In spite of Simmel's protestations to the contrary, modern philosophy passes through the flirt (*die Kokette*) in its encounter with its own finitude, just as ancient philosophy had passed through the figure of the sorceress.

RHETORIC'S FLIRTATION WITH LITERATURE, FROM GORGIAS TO ARISTOTLE: THE EPIDEICTIC GENRE

Rüdiger Campe

1

In flirting, seduction, one way or another, is in touch with its own possibility. Once such a process has taken hold, a startling alternative presents itself: Either seduction turns flirtatious in the parallel worlds of potentiality, or it becomes apparent that it has been its own potentiality that, from the beginning, provided a first hold for seduction to become effective. This means either that the art of flirtation is a Romantic theater where nothing is in fact what it seems or that it is only with the substratum of a stage that gestures acquire the meaning that then can or cannot have effects in the real world of seduction. In either case seduction can be said to entertain a flirtatious relation with flirtation. It either turns into the mirror of an aesthetic spectacle or relies on a flirtatious "prelude on the stage" (Goethe, *Faust*).

As much, or so it seems, can be said about what we call persuasion in rhetoric. In fact the erotic scenario lends itself to a convenient analogy that allows us to better understand a major conundrum in the theory and history of rhetoric. As seduction turns into the potentiality of flirtation in the double sense described, rhetorical persuasion can be said to turn virtual in aesthetics and literature (literature meaning here the art form of prose [*Kunstprosa*]);[1] alternately aesthetics and literature might even reveal themselves as the sources from which something like the effects of persuasion are only derived. Either literature is the aestheticized afterimage of rhetorical effects, or rhetorical effects, performative as well as pragmatic, imply the self-referential subset of literary figures in which rhetoric defines the potential of becoming effective in actual minds and souls.

The hypothesis in what follows is that epideixis—the rhetorical genre of praise—functions in this precise (double) sense as the aesthetic-literary moment within rhetoric. The analogy, however, as with every good metaphor, is informative only because praising beautiful bodies, brilliant deeds, and artful objects is of an erotic nature in itself and, as such, has been part of epideixis's own (pre)history. Even the analogy between rhetoric's relations to aesthetics and seduction's involvement with flirtation—the metaphorical value of flirtation—is, in the end, flirtatious.

2

Praise and blame take place among men and women. This is how Gorgias of Leontini starts the exordium in the *Praise of Helen*:

> The order proper [*kosmos*] to a city-state is being well-manned; to a body, beauty; to a soul, wisdom; to a deed, excellence; and to a discourse, truth—and the opposites of these are disorder. And the praiseworthy man and woman and discourse and work and city-state and deed one must honor with praise, while one must assign blame to the unworthy—for it is equal error to blame the praiseworthy and to praise the blameworthy.[2]

From *polis* to discourse, everything has its proper order: Being well equipped with man-power (*evandria*) gives essential *kosmos* to the city-state, just as truth (*aletheia*) is the *kosmos* to be expected with regard to *logos*. After this first phrase Gorgias peruses nearly the same enumeration of notions once more. This time, however, he substitutes the work (*ergon*) for the body and, even more important, reverses the sequence of the terms. He takes his departure now from *logos*, the term with which he ended in the first instance, and he concludes with deed (*pragma*) for a change. This second round replaces substantial entities from city to speech with the trajectory of human activities from speaking to acting. Accordingly it is no longer keyed by the rubric of *kosmos*, the order of things. Instead Gorgias now attributes to each member of the chain of terms its own claim to praise, and he makes it the essential *hamartia* in each case not to give the proper praise to the praiseworthy. Praise and blame make their appearance between these two sequences. They emerge between the order of things, from *polis* to *logos*, and the chain from mental to physical actions—between, in other words, an epic *kosmos* and a dramatic, possibly tragic potentiality of *hamartia*, a possibility that comes with the choices of acting. What is more, together with the difference between epic order and dramatic potentiality a quite different difference and relation emerge: the difference and relation between men and women. What then emerges with the emergence of praise or blame and men and women? Why are Gorgias's exemplary discourse and, later on, Iscocrates' famous response to it, speeches in the praise of Helen, the praise that is to refute the *hamartia* of false blame? This much is clear: Whatever in the world of entities and their *kosmos* or *akosmia* the seduction of either Paris or Helena (or both) means, it refers back to the choice of praising or blaming, and that means the potentiality of a dramatic *hamartia*.

Even if we recognize that the factual and thematic circumstances of the praise of Helen are a defining motif in the early history of rhetoric, something else is required to support such a motif and give it its structural importance. This support can be found in a very different beginning of praise in Greece, praise without names and choice this time, and without the alternative of blaming: the praise of the fallen in war. The funeral oration for the war dead seems to be, if not exclusively, then at least predominantly an Athenian invention and practice. Pericles' speech on the dead of the first year of war in Thucydides' *History of the Peloponnesian War* is the locus classicus. The epideixis, demonstration *ad oculos* and demonstrative argument at the same time, consists of three days of display of the dead bodies and their burial at a public grave site, followed by the speech of an orator. The orator has been chosen by and introduces himself in the name of the *polis*; he does not hold any office or position other than being chosen for the occasion.[3] This, it seems, is the latest stage in the historical development of rhetorical orations and their sites in Greece, and it is the one that is most explicitly institutionalized as a rhetorical act.[4] Juridical speech and speech at the agora are both code-veloped with the institutions and the related histories of law and trial. The *epitaphios* for the war dead is, by contrast, the institution of oration as such. It proceeds by making Athens itself its ultimate agent and recipient. Every name except that of Athens is blocked out in the speech: no mention of the commanding general, no names of men fighting and dying, not even of any sites or occasions of action in the course of which they were killed. Pericles, in Thucydides' presentation, also blocks out his own name: Chosen to carry out the oration, he would prefer to perform yet another—anonymous—action or work action (*ergon*) rather than the speech. When he has delivered the praise of the dead *kata ton nomon* (according to the law), he gives the voice back to the audience: He tells them to return to the city, "when you have, each single one of you, lamented the one whom to lament is appropriate to you."[5] Introduction of the speaker and dismissal of the audience thus institutionalize a "universal singular." On the one hand, there is the orator who erases his individuality in the name of the city, and on the other, there is the audience in which each member may perform a similar act of lamentation. It is in this framework that Pericles develops the famous picture of the Athenian *polis* as a whole out of independent singulars.

The *institutionalized* oration—the oration commissioned by the *polis*—is an *institutionalizing* oration. In this double relation with the institution, the speech imposes the space for further reinstitutionalization; the orator effaces himself and empowers the singularity of each member of the audience in order to circumscribe the very space in which his words can have the effect of public address. By presupposing itself as the possibility of rhetoric and its means and effects in their empirical heterodoxy, the institutionalized-institutionalizing oration is on its way to—but never entirely reaches—the point of systemic closure.

It may well be that this is what Gorgias demonstrated in his own *epitaphios*. But not enough survives for us to be sure. In the *Encomium of Helen*, in any event, Gorgias shows and exploits the institutionalized-institutionalizing logic. In that case, however, what is at stake is not the logic of the *polis* commissioning an act of rhetoric but of rhetoric commissioning itself as another form of poetry. Gorgias (and later Isocrates) thus incorporate the structure of institutionalization in the fabric of a praise of Helen, the seduction and its flirtatious grounds in praise or blame of man and woman.

This is an outline of how Gorgias's *Encomium* proceeds: As becomes clear in the exordium, praise hovers between positively stating the person or thing to be praised to possess the proper *kosmos*, on the one hand, and correcting the *hamartia* of blaming the praiseworthy, on the other. Such is, according to the *Encomium*, the situation of Helen. Born of gods as the most beautiful of all women (with beauty being the *kosmos* proper to the body), Helen is the emblematic target of blame for having caused the Trojan War (the work or *ergon* that, by a *hamartia*, exposes the praiseworthy to blame). In this latter respect each attempt to praise Helen is built, as it were, over an Athenian funeral oration. And it is for having refuted the blame that Gorgias states in conclusion, "I tried to put an end to the injustice of blame and ignorance of opinion [*doxes amathia*]."[6]

Praising Helen thus requires not only positive praise but also and importantly the refutation of the false blame by all those who accuse her of having caused what destroyed the lives of many men. The poets and their adherence to the myth are at the origin of both the positive praise of Helen's godly nature and the false blame of being guilty of the Trojan War. Refuting the lie of the poets while maintaining the truth of the myth seems a variation of sorts on the Platonic theme of the critique of poetry and myth in the *Republic.* More precisely, for Gorgias to show Helen's innocence amounts to making the argument that she was not responsible for being married to Paris. "Either by the wishes of Fortune and plans of the gods and decrees of Necessity she did what she did, or abducted by force, or persuaded by speeches, [or conquered by Love]."[7] In all of these cases (an obviously complete set for Gorgias) he goes on to show Helen not being the responsible party. The cases of mere fortune and irrefutable necessity are, according to the author of the *Encomium,* as easily demonstrated as the case of love. In every one of these scenarios Helen appears obviously not being the one responsible for the "work." All the emphasis in Gorgias's discussion is on the "persuasion by speeches" (*logois peistheisa*). This point is at the same time the subject matter of the *Encomium* in its entirety. Presenting persuasive discourse, Gorgias argues, "shapes [*etyposato*] the soul at will."[8] This is possible since men are lacking attention to things past, present, and future; they lack, in other words, the force and reliability of memory, awareness, and foreknowledge. Opinion, *doxa,* is what "shapes the soul," on account of the soul's weakness with regard to such forms of administering attention to sense perception and thinking. The force of lying in persuasive discourse is therefore irrefutable for the soul that is necessarily shaped by it. Persuasion erases the responsibility of she who is persuaded by he who persuades. In short, demonstrating that poets are lying about Helen when they blame her for the Trojan War finally requires showing that lying discourse is irrefutable when exercised on a soul that constitutively lacks attention to things past, present, and future. By demonstrating the irrefutable power of (poetic) persuasion, the blaming of the praiseworthy is refuted and, by the same token, proper praise is accomplished.

Since praising Helen requires refuting the false blame of the poets, and the blame of the poets is false because of the persuasive speech to which Helen is exposed by the poets, Helen's praise implies belief in, and thereby confirms, the force of praise and persuasive speech as its own—mythical-poetic—ground. By praising Helen, the object of persuasive praise par excellence, praise constructs its own potentiality. Such potentiality then is something like a proto-persuasive, namely poetically persuasive, speech. The truth is that the poets not only lie but lie persuasively. The essence of persuasively lying discourse is identified by Gorgias not as figurative speech in prose but as poetry: "Discourse having meter I suppose and name (in the general sense) to be poetry. Fearful shuddering and tearful pity and sorrowful longing come upon those who hear it, and the soul experiences a peculiar feeling, on account of the words, at the good and bad fortunes of other people's affairs and bodies."[9] It is the poetic account of "the good and bad fortunes of other people's affairs and bodies" that informs, within persuasive address, the very element that makes it a lie, and an irrefutable lie at that. Helen, it may be concluded from the *Encomium*—though Gorgias never describes any such scene—hears Paris speaking to herself as if "by incantation" and praising a woman called Helen, the daughter of gods and most beautiful of women. In the activity of praise, rhetoric institutionalizes itself by means of self-implication while referring to its mirror image in poetry, a realm in which opinion-induced effects erase the other's responsibility by mere incantation.

"By this discourse," so Gorgias concludes, "I have removed infamy from a woman. . . . I tried to put an end to the injustice of blame and ignorance of opinion; I wanted to write this discourse, an encomium for Helen and a plaything for myself." Reference to its own potential grounding—a grounding in poetic incantation—is proper to the praise of Helen. By praising Helen persuasive speech in Gorgias repeats that which in Thucydides' account had once been accomplished by the anonymity of the *epitaphios*.

3

With the genre of praise, persuasive speech retraces its own institutionalization. This can be understood in two different and yet supplementary ways. It can mean, first, that rhetoric becomes

reinstitutionalizing. This happens when the speech, as with Pericles, reestablishes the institution, which commissioned it in the first
place. Such is the case of the encomium proper and its historical
locus, the "general singular" of the funeral oration for those who
died in war. This monumental reinstitutionalizing effect of public
speech in the *polis* is mimicked and duplicated as it were by a second, *deinstitutionalizing* persuasive speech. Such an effect takes
place when the speech identifies in itself the trope of poetry that
argues for its own functioning and application. This happens not
coincidentally in a praise of Helen, a speech that is related to the
paradigmatic instance of seduction and the flirtatious potentiality of
praise or blame.

Even if it must remain open which of the two accounts—the reinstitutionalization or the deinstitutionalization—is the more appropriate explication in Greek literary history,[10] the two forms of encomium
and their relation to each other can in any event be brought together
with Ernst Robert Curtius's remarks on the *genos epideiktikon* in *European Literature and the Latin Middle Ages.* Gorgias, Curtius argues on the one hand, "is the first master of epideictic oratory, and
that means of an ancient *Kunstprosa,* artistic prose." On the other
hand, Curtius states, "Epideictic speech has been by far most influ-
ential on medieval poetry."[11] This proves a fundamental paradox in
what is, in the broad historical perspective of Curtius, the relation
between rhetoric and literature (or prose as a form of art, an aesthetic object). Epideixis, Curtius tells us, informs the advent of literature in a double movement: It projects the rhetorical-poetical qualities of artful composition onto prose, language without form, from
the beginning of Greek rhetoric on, *and* it increasingly retransforms
poetry, formed language par excellence, into rhetoric. Finally the epideictic is all that remains of rhetoric when the genres of forensic rhetoric and political speech, the institutional forms of rhetoric in the
primary understanding, cease to exist in imperial Rome. It is through
the pseudo-institutional effect of praise that rhetoric survives itself
and, in its eternal afterlife, turns into something called "literature."

Such a double characteristic of the epideictic, however, implies a situation in which it has become, in its peculiar positioning with public speech and persuasion, part and parcel of and even constitutive for rhetoric. The development can be observed in Aristotle's *Art of Rhetoric*. The Helen theme as well as its counterpoint, the anonymous praise of the fallen in war, turn latent here. They disappear from the surface to the extent that the epideictic definitively enters the fabric of the art of rhetoric and its defining three genres. With this move the analogical and structural importance of the seduction-flirtation relationship—as suggested in the first section of this paper—finally takes hold for rhetoric. In its relations with the agonistic genres of juridical and political speech—and the seduction mode of persuasion—the epideictic *is* now, in the fabric of the rhetorical system, the flirtatious, potentiality-bound ground of rhetorical persuasion. And in this systemic relationship of the two agonistic genres with the genre of praise and blame we recognize a foreshadowing of the future, transrhetorical, relation between rhetoric and literature. Providing more evidence for this claim is the goal of the rest of this paper.

In Aristotle's account the famous triad of the juridical, the deliberative (political), and the epideictic genres is instituted for centuries to come. The epideictic form is eccentric vis-à-vis the triadic whole of rhetorical genres under a number of rubrics, and yet it is only through its being added to juridical speech and speech at the agora that a system of rhetorical technicality can be formulated in the first place. It is under this double perspective that epideixis proves to be rhetoric's flirtation with literature within rhetoric. The genres of juridical and political speech both take their departure from institutional frameworks that predate rhetoric in the social world: Juridical speech relies on the development of the trial and its procedures, whereas political speech harks back to constitutional law and political practices. The world-structures, which we must assume to exist in order for the procedures and practices of juridical and political rhetoric to be effective, are, retroactively, conditioned on those same

procedures and practices. With its institutional embedding, political
and juridical rhetoric discloses that kind of a world—the world of opinion or passion—which then gives rhetoric its power to produce effects in people's minds and souls. Heidegger, in his seminar on Aristotle and the commentary on rhetoric in particular, privileged the
political genre, and *doxa* as its characteristic element.[12] One may argue that juridical speech, in Aristotle's account of it, offers an even
more pertinent example. In this case it is *pathos* as a rhetorical category that is specifically linked to the scene of argumentation before the court.[13] However we further develop such implications of
rhetoric—implications that retroactively make accessible the structure
of a world in which rhetoric unfolds as an effect-producing techne—
epideictic speech proves to be of a clearly different nature. The epideictic genre deinstitutionalizes rhetorical speech through the self-
implying, quasi-institutional character of praise. Three rubrics are to
be discussed with regard to the epideictic genre's special and potentially transgressive place in rhetoric: temporality, the addressee, and
the medium of presentation.[14]

  1. *Temporality.* To each of the three genres of rhetoric, Aristotle
notes, "a special time [*chronos*] is appropriate: to the deliberative,
the future; for the speaker, whether he exhorts or dissuades, always
advises about things to come; to the forensic, the past; for it is always in reference to things done that one party accuses and the other
defends; to the epideictic, most appropriately the present [*ho parion*];
for it is the existing condition of things [*ta hyparchonta*] that all those
who praise or blame have in view."[15] Given the interpretation of the
present in the epideictic, it is appropriate to assume that "time" is
meant here in two different ways. Both forensic and political speech
might be said to employ grammatical tenses with a referential meaning. When the defendant and the accuser use the past tense, they both
mean the past. The orator on the agora speaking in the future tense
refers to a scenario in the future. The present of the epideictic, however, is the present of that which, in the moment of our speaking, is
there for us to use or to misuse, to actualize or not. People and things

are called *ta hyparchonta* inasmuch as they are there for the speaker to turn to them; they are the possible material of his speech. With the epideictic the grammatical tense of the present thus does not function referentially but rather indicates things and living beings as existing beyond temporality and thus as ready to appear in discourse. This specificity of the epideictic present further unfolds with the following two points.

2. *Addressee.* "The hearer," says Aristotle, "must necessarily be either a mere spectator [*theoros*] or a judge [*krites*], and a judge either of things past or of things to come. For instance, a member of the general assembly is a judge of things to come; the dicast [*dikastes*: 'the judge in the proper sense,' 'the judge at court'], of things past; the mere spectator, of the ability of the speaker [(krinou) peri tes dynameos]."[16] One may translate these last words also as "the spectator's judgment on potentiality," which then can be the potentiality of the speaker (as assumed in the translation), of the art of rhetoric, or even of the things addressed in rhetorical speech. Being addressed by speech can mean, first, to hear, through the mediation of speech, of things that possess actuality, things that are happening and having actual effect in the world. Such actuality can only be something that either has happened (the deed of wrongdoing) or that is going to happen (the scenario of political deliberation). Second, being the addressee of speech can also mean to actually attend something, being the *theoros* or spectator of something. This applies characteristically to epideixis, and only to epideixis. What has actual presence for the *theoros* in epideictic speech is the very appearance of the speech; in its presentness this speech manifests a *dynamis*, potential or potentiality, namely, the potential or potentiality of rhetoric to perform the work of rhetoric or, finally, of persons and things to unfold their potential for demonstrating might, beauty, or excellence.

Only by understanding the juxtaposition of judge and spectator in such a strictly complementary way, and only by giving *dynamis* its metaphysical implication, that of potentiality, does it seems possible to do justice to Aristotle's insistence on having exhausted all

possible cases of being addressed by speech "with necessity." The epideictic thus withdraws from the world of judgment and reported actuality to a presentness that is precisely the experience of potentiality. This is the first strict sense in which rhetoric can be said to flirt
with literature.

3. *Media.* In Book III, the book on elocution, Aristotle juxtaposes
two styles: *lexis graphike*, the written style, and *lexis agonistike*, the
style of antagonistic debate. "But we must not lose sight of the fact
that a different style is suitable to each kind of Rhetoric. That of written composition is not the same as that of debate; nor, in the latter,
is that of public speaking the same as that of the law courts."[17] For
quite some time the text of Aristotle's lecture on rhetoric holds back
as to where exactly to find instances of such *lexis graphike*. The genres
of forensic speech and public address occupy the foreground as the
first and foremost genres of the—oral—*agon*. Only in the last para-
graph of this section, dealing with style in general, is the implica-
tion finally made explicit: "The epideictic style is especially suited to
written composition [*lexis graphikotate*], for its function [*ergon*] is
reading [*anagnosis*]."[18] It is easy to see how the somewhat mysteri-
ous characterizations of the epideictic with regard to the *theoros* (spectator) and the split between tense and referential time find their explanation in the theorem of reading. The spectator turns out to be a
reader, and what he looks at, it might be argued, is a text instead of
a speech.[19] The split between temporal meaning and grammatical
tenses can be interpreted as the characteristic temporality of reading. The temporal experience of the reading process encompasses
the tenses but is not identical with them. For the spectator who is a
reader all tenses can be called present in the sense of the *hyparchonta*,
that is, of that which is at his disposal as a reader. Finally the *dynamis* (of the speaker, of rhetoric as such, or even of the entities and
people in the world as unfolding qualities for possible "demonstration"), which is the object of this spectator's judgment, can be seen
in light of his being a reader. As an object of reading, the words of
the epideictic text turn out to belong to the sphere of *dynamis* rather

than that of *energeia* or *actualitas*. What the spectator of the epideictic text "sees" by looking at its words is the potentiality in or behind them: the potentiality of the one who wrote them, the forms of
composition employed, or even of the people and things shown in
those words. Literature appears, in rhetoric and beyond rhetoric, as
the potentiality of what is read.

Certainly a full-blown theory of reading as assumed in the last remarks may not yet be available in Aristotle.[20] The emphasis in this
section of the *Art of Rhetoric* resides in the seemingly oblique juxtaposition of written style and agon-related style. Writing and reading
are not so much seen as medial forms that are different from oral
delivery or extemporization, nor are *agon* and the placid pleasure
of being a spectator pitched directly against each other. Rather it is
the *agon*—which happens to require orality—that is juxtaposed
with writing and reading, which, for their part, exclude any *agon*
and favor mere pleasure. The opposition lies between the strife of
the *agon*, which implicates us in the absent forms of past and future
actualities, and the process of reading, which in its turn presents us
with the potentiality of that which is at our disposal as readers. As
something accomplished in the *agon* persuasion occurs as actual
seduction; in the "most writerly style," the style of the epideictic which
the reader as a *theoros* looks at, persuasion flirtatiously plays with
potentiality—the potentiality of the writer, the means of persuasion,
or its effects in the world. This, in the end, means that, by turning
theoros or reader, the "judge" of the epideictic text flirts with rhetoric's future as literature.

4

With this last observation the brief exploration on the epideictic comes
full circle to where it began. Aesthetics and literature—this was the
point of departure—is to rhetoric what flirtation is to seduction. The
erotics of praise—the praise of the beautiful in particular but also
of the mighty or the rich, the noble or the ingenious, the praise of

potentiality—has turned out to be the mode of rhetoric flirting with the aesthetics of literature, the flirt with flirtation.

An ironic footnote to this comes from Quintilian. In the *Institutio oratoria* Helen and her praise resurface in the context of the epideictic genre. The potentiality of the epideictic here appears with doubt cast about the potency in potentiality. In the *Institutio oratoria* Helen reemerges as the object of praise under the rubric of *auxesis*, the figure of stylistic intensification and enlargement.[21] Under this rubric Quintilian refers to the praise of Helen's beauty by the old and wise men of Troy instead of the youthful and vigorous, to the praise of Helen, one might say, by Priamus instead of Paris. The augmenting nature of this praise and its *topoi* lie for Quintilian in its deviation from the ordinary purpose. There is no good reason for the old and wise to praise the beauty of Helen, who caused so much misery for the city. Their praise of Helen not only uses devices of augmentation; it is nothing other than augmentation. It is the flirtatious purpose without purposes of those who have nothing to gain.

All the features of the Aristotelian proto-literary theory of the epideictic are present in the *Institutio oratoria*: the spectator-judge who trades pleasure for real-world decisions, the peculiar presentness of the genre and its close connection with reading. And yet alongside all these Aristotelian features the faint remembrance of earlier days reemerges as well, a remembrance of the times of praise and persuasion with the sophists, of seduction and flirtation as they are related to the praise of Helen. After Aristotle's constitutive reinterpretation of rhetoric, it is now the old men who wisely engage in the praise of Helen's beauty. By doing so, however, they form the avantgarde of rhetoric's flirtation with what even in Quintilian's days still lies ahead, the aesthetic object of the work of literature.

PLAYING WITH YOURSELF: ON
THE SELF-REFERENCE OF FLIRTATION

Arne Höcker

1

To make yourself attractive to somebody it may appear helpful at times to induce jealousy by making eyes at someone else. I will therefore for now resist Rüdiger Campe's generous offer and first engage instead with Paul Fleming's contribution to this volume. In the concluding section of his essay, Fleming presents us with the *Odyssey*'s episode of the song of the Sirens as the primal scene of flirtation as art and art as flirtation. Keeping himself at a distance while enjoying the beautiful forces of brute seduction and temptation, Odysseus becomes "the great resister, *the one who converts seduction to flirtation*," Fleming writes. And "like all true flirters," he concludes, "Odysseus gets it all by getting nothing." I would like to confront this poetic primal scene of flirtation with a text from the other end of literary history, where the two-thousand-year-old literary tradition of unfolding the possibilities of fictionalization, according to David Wellbery, comes to an end.[1] In a small prose piece from 1917, Kafka rewrites Odysseus's encounter with the Sirens, who in Kafka's interpretation make use of a weapon even deadlier than their song:

remaining silent. It is questionable in Kafka's story whether Odysseus, who had apparently been convinced to listen to the alluring song, was just pretending. However, I will not offer another in-depth analysis of the often analyzed story and will not further engage in the unanswerable question of whether Odysseus truly failed to hear the silence of the Sirens. But something else catches one's attention when rereading Kafka's short prose piece under the premises of flirtation: Not only do the Sirens refuse to sing for Odysseus, who nevertheless believes in and enjoys being the object of seduction. In fact the Sirens themselves surrender to the seductive forces of flirtation; Odysseus's art of self-deception and self-esteem are just too attractive not to fall for: "But they—lovelier than ever—stretched their necks and turned, let their awesome hair flutter free in the wind, and freely stretched their claws on the rocks. They no longer had any desire to allure; all that they wanted was to hold as long as they could the radiance that fell from Ulysses' great eyes."[2]

Here Kafka offers two relevant insights into the logic of flirtation. First, there is the almost hidden aspect of temporality, the desire to extend the present moment, to remain enthralled by the enthrallment of the other. But it should not be forgotten that the Sirens were silent and that Odysseus's gaze was fixed on the horizon, stuck in a comforting sphere of an imaginary present. In this respect flirtation appears as the presence of deferral, as a desire and even an attempt to make permanent the suspenseful moment on the threshold of an event, where nothing has happened yet, but everything is still possible. In Kafka's short piece Odysseus and the Sirens share the joy of the present moment, in which expectations and wishes persist in a state of *fulfillability*.

Second, Kafka reminds us here that flirtation is a quiet, even silent activity. While the song is supposed to seduce, flirtation is characterized by an exchange of gazes or indeed glimpses (*Augenblicke*), which are fleeting, elusive, and transient. Gazes, however, need to be read. One must interpret and guess what they mean, particularly when a gaze responds to a gaze that itself is based on the interpreta-tion of a gaze. As many know from painful experience, the magic of flirtation often ceases when someone opens his or her mouth. What can be concluded from this short Kafka reading can be summarized thus: To seduction belongs speech and song—let us say rhetoric. To flirtation belongs reading and writing; in the context of this book that means literature.

2

This is precisely the distinction that is at stake in Campe's essay on rhetoric's flirtation with literature. In his contribution, with which I will now engage more intimately, Campe investigates the historical process in which rhetoric prefigures the possibility of literature by self-institutionalizing the institution of rhetoric. In what follows I do not want to merely repeat or even attempt to summarize Campe's essay. Instead I would like to try to further elaborate on its relevance for an overall theory of flirtation. To that effect we should recall the three instances where rhetoric converges with literature in the rhe-torical genre of praise that Campe has outlined: the temporality of the present, the convergence of judge and spectator as close readers of texts, and textuality and the specificity of writing.

It is the epideictic genre and its precursors, the *epitaphios* and the *encomium*, that Campe identifies as the specific genre in which rhetoric converges or *flirts* with literature. In contrast to the two other rhetorical genres—the forensic and the deliberative genres, with their distinct institutional frameworks—the epideictic genre frames and in-stitutionalizes itself as rhetoric. It is this particular self-referentiality that Campe characterizes as a process of de- and reinstitutionaliza-tion, and one is tempted to call it a kind of reentry of rhetoric.[3] But how does this relate to the art of flirtation? Campe uses flirtation less as a concept than as a metaphor that contributes to a better under-standing of "a major conundrum in the theory and history of rhetoric."

He also refers to the particularly erotic nature of the epideictic genre by which the analogy between rhetoric/seduction and aesthetics/flirtation appears itself to be flirtatious. I would like to make this supposition the point of departure for engaging with Campe's argument. Therefore we need to return once again to the starting point of his discussion. In his famous *Encomium of Helen* the sophist Gorgias praises Helen by defending her against those who blame her for being the cause of the Trojan War. And he does so not by judging her actions but by approaching the encomium as a logical exercise of—one could say—interpretation or discourse. What Gorgias seems to argue is that Helen has been seduced, which requires a certain force—such as the persuasive force of rhetorical discourse. Gorgias seems to reach his goal of praising Helen when he has successfully proven that she could not become the object of blame as she cannot be held responsible for the violent force that was done to her. Concluding his encomium, Gorgias could write what every chivalrous gentleman desires to claim: "By this discourse, I have removed infamy from a woman."[4] But as Campe and others before him have emphasized,[5] this was not the only goal of Gorgias's endeavor. He also simply wanted to write the discourse, the encomium itself, and he wanted to write it "as a plaything for myself."[6]

This emphasis on the encomium as a goal and a *plaything for myself* attests to a certain self-sufficiency of the discourse that has no other external purpose. Furthermore *plaything* seems to be a fine word to characterize a certain aspect of flirtation as a matter of less serious consequence or—maybe better—a matter that approaches itself consciously as a game and is therefore aware of its conditions of possibility and its own means. But one could go even further with this analogy. The plaything in Gorgias's encomium is indeed the other side of seduction. Moreover, set out as a plaything, the *Encomium of Helen* exposes its own rhetorical modus and turns against discourse that uses seductive and persuasive force in order to cause certain effects. In this context Campe suggests looking at rhetoric's flirtation with literature as a process of de- and reinstitutionalization, a process of self-institutionalization or self-empowerment. Or, with a Nietzschean spin, the institutionalization of literature as the truth of the lie of rhetoric.

3

We should revisit here the three instances that Campe identifies as the epideictic genre's transgressive potential in rhetoric: temporality, addressee, and medium. Following Aristotle's account of the three genres of rhetoric, Campe argues that epideixis can be seen as the very place where rhetoric turns into literature. This is the case because epideixis becomes the testing ground for rhetorical form: Under the framing conditions of praise, rhetoric itself can be observed and its specific techniques systematically recorded. Its time of reference being the present, the addressee of epideictic speech is not considered a judge of things past or those to come but is directly confronted with the dynamics of the speech that appears right before his or her eyes. It is not very difficult to see how this spectator of epideictic speech turns out to be a reader and how epideictic speech therefore turns out to be written text.

One further conclusion becomes possible that has not yet been discussed sufficiently and that brings us back to the very beginning of this commentary. If the epideictic genre can be seen as the exploration of what is possible in rhetoric, its mode is indeed that of a game, and its point of reference fiction. Once again this is what the self-referential ending of Gorgias's *Encomium of Helen* shows. In her reading of the *Encomium*, Elisabeth Strowick has shown that the emphasis on praise as "plaything" reveals the rhetoricity not only of the encomium but also of Helen as its object. The truth about Helen, Strowick concludes, is a product of rhetorical speech that therefore functions not as a form of representation but as a performative act.[7] Within rhetoric, that is to say, the epideictic genre explores the possibilities

of fictionalization, and this allows us not only to read it as literature
but also to claim its metaphorical proximity to flirtation.

4

To conclude I would like to suggest a reversal of perspective and to
have a look at flirtation through the lens of literature. What should
we consider the conditions of possibility of flirtation? Most important, and as is certainly true for every game, one needs to know
how to play, to understand the rules. In the case of flirtation this refers to socially accepted forms of communication, the common use of
culturally developed codes that transmit information on a basis of selection and thus guarantee connectivity. What makes flirtation so attractive, in our context and as such, is that it breaks down the societal
codification of erotic or amorous encounters and turns it into a playful procedure by which these codes engage with their own possibilities. Thus flirtation defines a transitional space, in which the use of
codes relates neither to failure nor to success and in which the game
refers solely to its own contingency and eventfulness. Something could
happen, and it is this very possibility that those involved in flirtation
experience and enjoy. Every step in the procedure of flirtation is eval-
uated, not by its value as illusion or reality in the world but by its
real effects within the game. The result, however, is a certain open-
ness with the potential to derive reality from fiction.

In this respect flirtation follows rules similar to those of literature.
This does not come as a surprise, as it is well known that the codes
in matters of love have essentially been transmitted by novelistic literature since the seventeenth century. It is on this literary history
that Niklas Luhmann bases his investigation into the codification of
love in *Love as Passion*, which one could read as the birth of flirtation from the literarization of seduction:

> Codification becomes reflected in the semantics of love at a much earlier
> stage than in other media of communication as a direct consequence of

printing. Even the early parodies of the novel themselves play a role in this context. Already by the seventeenth century it was common knowledge that the lady had read novels and therefore knew the code. This enhanced her attentiveness. She was forewarned—and endangered precisely by that very fact. Somewhat later, the sensitive male also became a victim of the novel. Everyone else had also read the clichés and gestures which were all part of the art of seduction. One cannot help but assume that the woman could see through them, but also knew that they would still be effective. The code thus not only regulated behaviour, but also documented its own recurrence in the very area of behaviour it regulated.[8]

I would like to end this essay on this note of self-referentiality. However, it should at least be mentioned that literature has of course returned rhetoric's offer to flirt. This can be learned from a remark that Luhmann makes in the beginning of his book regarding the choice of literary texts for his study: "I made a point of looking for second- and third-rate literature, and allowed myself to be guided by a very subjective principle in selecting quotations, namely, that of stylistic elegance."[9]

FLIRTATION WITH THE WORLD

STAGING APPEAL, PERFORMING AMBIVALENCE

Lauren Shizuko Stone

Flirtation's relation to seduction might be thought of as citational; it borrows the gesture, the performance, and the language, but it also retains a difference. In doing so, however, it might also reveal something unstable in seduction's own character. To develop this notion of flirtation vis-à-vis seduction, I'd like to consider the ordinary circumstances in which such a distinction might arise, such as those that happen in quotidian spaces: in bars, in offices, and on sidewalks. Let me begin by suggesting that, broadly speaking, seduction has an aim that establishes a distinct relationship of power—social, sexual, intellectual power. To offer a few classic arrangements: We might feel ourselves seduced by that one who politically outranks us or whose charm arrives through torridly witty prose. Or perhaps, with our own physical grace or prowess, we might be the ones using our sex appeal to seduce the unsuspecting. This asymmetry is evident in each scenario. Just as an artful production works to captivate its audience, this is the staging of appeal: a test of one's gravitational pull. In any case it quickly reveals itself as something that mobilizes (or at least is an attempt to mobilize) a form of subjective dominance. The language of seduction thus transposes the harmless staging of desire into a scene of danger: The audience is suddenly vulnerable to advances; one's affection can be captured; indeed we often invoke the passive voice to describe that certain powerlessness in the face of successful intersubjective maneuvers: "to have been seduced."

So what then is flirtation? Does the flirter really want to get the "flirtee" into bed? Does the flirtation end—or cease to be flirtation at all—if they exchange phone numbers? Or rather, in a moment of mutuality, are both parties simultaneously flirter and flirtee? The answers here must be *yes* and *no*; indeed flirtation in this way hinges first on failure of a certain kind, but a failure that must arrive beforehand. If the intent is to get the other into bed, well, that is seduction. So the successful flirtation involves only the activity of the tease, the charm, indeed the play, and all with the precise purpose of failing to ever fully enrapture the other. It thus requires a form of equality on desire's stage, where flirtation circumvents the imbalance of the seducer vis-à-vis the seduced in that, to flirt effectively, someone must always be flirting back. So is it just a game, a kind of play, a codified but otherwise "empty gesture"? Indeed games are just as likely to deploy a familiar sense of power, opposition, winning and losing—so it cannot be a game, strictly speaking. If it is a playing-at, a well-mannered rehearsal, or the play-acting of desire itself, then flirtation certainly must be drawing from a source external to itself. Recalling Judith Butler, perhaps we could consider flirtation to be a form of citation—and in borrowing from the lexicon of seduction, its offerings always come with a wink, as if to simultaneously announce: "This is *not* seduction."

If, however, this seduction that is *not* seduction must be thought of as decoupled from the stakes of dominance and submission, I would still urge caution against flatly declaring flirtation to be merely a form of "castrated" or "virginal" (unconsummated) seduction. If the contours of flirtation are specifically identifiable *against* seduction (in keeping with the notion of its loose citationality), then flirtation, especially that sort of shameless flirting—we might say flirting with abandon—could be rephrased as being the "drag" of staged desire.

Butler notes that, with respect to gender, "drag implicitly reveals the imitative structure . . . as well as its contingency." The "giddiness" that results from such a performance is, on her view, precisely the revelation that "anatomical sex, gender identity, and gender performance" are only culturally constituted and, where there is any apparent unity, neither "natural" nor "necessary." On Butler's view drag thrills by throwing open the curtain: The citational performance does not underscore rigid connections between bodily sex and concepts of "woman" or "man" as parody, but rather the parody points precisely toward the way the performance of "woman" or "man" is all there is.[1]

Analogically flirtation can be also understood to be a troublemaker for any unflinching view of seduction's legibility; flirtation's relation to seduction is thus not purely imitative. Each of the ordinary scenarios I have outlined here—making a pass at the office or a wink at the bar—belong to both flirtation and seduction. From the outward perspective (i.e., expressions or acts), in themselves such gestures, lexica, and performances are virtually indistinguishable. Is the coy look from across the room merely part of the tease or the prelude to more? Its determination as flirtation is not immediately legible as it falls under intent; for it to play out as a flirtation both players must be willing to be flirter and flirtee, thus avoiding the power differential already suggested. But for flirtation to be titillating—and here we see its affinity to drag—there is a contingency that is also made visible. If flirtation is to be any fun at all the parties involved cannot mutually and explicitly agree in advance that this will be an "act"; rather they revel in the open futurity. Indeed one never knows quite what the other wants or intends.[2] The thrill or "giddiness" here arrives because, in both flirtation and seduction, there is no "necessary" connection between the outward performance and the inner attitude.

Flirtation is thus not a paltry imitation of seduction; it rests on the same principles of contingency, of invisible and malleable intent. It is, in a Butlerean sense, however, a parody—it is seduction in drag—insofar as the pleasure we receive from flirtation does not point to a relation of strict mimesis (imitating seduction—what fun is that?) but uncovers the shared and essential instability that undergirds both.

LIFE IS A FLIRTATION: THOMAS MANN'S *FELIX KRULL*

Elisabeth Strowick

If one wanted to describe the forms of flirtation depicted in *Felix Krull* in a concise formula, one might use a phrase that comes from Felix Krull himself: "Forays upon the sweets of life [Griffe in die Süßigkeiten des Lebens]."[1] The talk is of such "forays" in that noteworthy scene in the delicatessen shop, from which Krull brings the "almost always" "abundant store" (C 40) of sweets to his "desk" (C 40). What this formula for flirtation implies is twofold: First, flirtation is taken out of the context of interpersonal relationships and opened up to become an aesthetic concept of life; second, to the extent that in *Felix Krull* it is impossible to separate life from the autobiographical project, the act of writing itself can be read as flirtation. This essay traces out each aspect of this framework: the performance, epistemology, and temporality of the "forays upon the sweets of life" as well as the "appetite" articulated in them and its consequences with respect to an aesthetics of perception.

The delicious presents itself as something atmospheric. One noontime Krull unexpectedly finds himself alone in the delicatessen store, empty not only of other customers but also of attendants. The description presents the "sweets of life" in a structurally infinite stringing-together:

> There were rows and rows of hams and sausages . . . —white, yellow, red, and black; fat and lean and round and long—rows of canned preserves, cocoa and tea, bright translucent glass bottles of honey, marmalade, and jam; round bottles and slender bottles, filled with liqueurs and punch—all these things crowded every inch of the shelves from top to bottom. Then there were glass showcases where smoked mackerel, lampreys, flounders, and eels were displayed on platters to tempt the appetite. . . . Artichokes, bundles of asparagus, truffles, little liver sausages in silver paper—all these things lay heaped in rich profusion; while on other tables stood open tin boxes full of fine biscuits, spice cakes piled in criss-cross layers, and glass urns full of dessert candies and candied fruits. (C 41–42)[2]

What the indulging gaze apprehends in this allegorical scene is nothing less than life itself—life as a delicacy that "presents itself." The syntax is one of appetite—a meandering from one to the next—and even when appetite is alluded to as a physiological dimension ("My mouth literally began to water like a spring" [C 42]), it is nonetheless a distinctly aesthetic experience, which is staged—in the words of Lacan—as an "appetite of the eye."[3] The fleeting or flirting gaze produces surfaces of enjoyment. The showcases of the delicatessen find continuation in the shop windows in Frankfurt, whose luxurious displays are stations—again strung together syntactically—in the journey of "education" (C 76) of curious onlookers. They are not so much displays of luxury goods as explicitly "enticing, educational aspects of the world" (C 79).[4] In other words they are presentations of the world, of life as a "rich profusion" (C 43), as "visual joys" (C 81).

The aesthetic manufacturing of reality, of life is an educational as well as artistic project: the "gift of seeing" is "an instructive gift" (C 79); the roaming eye, bearer of the aesthetic education of a life that is "based on imagination and self-discipline" (C 51). For Felix Krull, like Gustav von Aschenbach, self-discipline and imagination nevertheless enter into a particular relationship where moderation is both constitutive of enjoyment and attained through it. In the repeated visits to the delicatessen shop, Krull takes "whatever was available, never shamelessly, but rather choosing moderately" (C 44), and in matters of love as well it is the alliance of enjoyment and discipline that leads to "refinement," to a "refinement . . . *through* love" (C 117). Krull is a "lover . . . of the world" (C 48), not of women. It is not grat-ification but desire that characterizes the "many kinds of satisfaction finer and more subtle" (C 48),[5] which might be appropriately denoted as *appetite* or *flirtation*.

"Imagination and self-discipline" are interlaced with the artistic act, with the "creative task [Schöpfung]" (C 37), or more precisely with the creating of reality. The illnesses that Krull repeatedly stages, for example, are such creations of reality that result from imagina-tion and "self-conquest"(C 40): "I had improved upon nature, real-ized a dream; and only he who has succeeded in creating a compel-ling and effective reality out of nothing . . . , out of nothing more than imagination and the daring exploitation of his own body—he alone understands the strange and dreamlike satisfaction with which I rested from my creative task" (C 36).[6]

Felix Krull is an "artist's novel" in the sense that it outlines an aes-thetics of life, an aesthetics of existence. Reality itself becomes the "scene" (C 42)—a scene that itself reflects on the (perceptive-)aesthetic manufacturing of reality—and the "appetite of the eye": The "pictures stirring desire" are distinguished by their "unimportance," their "in-significance," "incidents of which nothing comes." Indeed Krull says, "It was nothing, it was only charming" (C 79).[7] It would be difficult to describe the reality effect of flirtation more precisely.

Krull's aesthetics of flirtation finds an epistemological correspon-dence in Freud's concept of the perception-consciousness system. "For, on our hypothesis," Freud writes in his short text *Negation*, "percep-tion is not a purely passive process. The ego periodically sends out small amounts of cathexis into the perceptual system, by means of which it samples the external stimuli, and then after every such tentative advance it draws back again."[8] Freud not only highlights the active role of sensory perception; he also uses formulations such as "tasting," "touching," and "feeler," which reveal perception to be a matter of appetite, and perhaps of flirtation. "Interruption" and "discontinuity"[9] are the structural condition for such a desire in the aesthetics of perception. Similarly Krull's "forays upon the sweets of life" do not take place "often nor regularly, but after a longer or shorter interval" (C 44), and the chronicling of his life also does not occur without interruptions.

Flirtation's aesthetics of perception produces reality as a scene, as a rhythmically appealing nothingness in which reality is constituted from its other. The chocolates that come from the delicatessen become "sweets of life" since they are what remains from dreams *in* reality ("as though left over from the dream" [C 43]): "They were of the best quality, those candies . . . ; but it was not alone their quality that enchanted me; even more it was the carrying over of my dream treasure into my waking life that made up the sum of my delight—a delight too great for me not to think of repeating it when occasion offered" (C 43–44). What is delicious is the (repeated) production of reality as a trace of a dream. There are numerous such traces that constitute the life of Felix Krull and thus also the Marquis de Venosta's offer to have him go on a journey in his place and with a suitably altered name and ennobled status, which enables Krull to unexpectedly realize one of his childhood dreams:

> How inventive life is! Lending substance to airy nothings it brings our childhood dreams to pass. Had not I in boyhood tasted in imagination those delights of incognito I fully savoured now, as I continued to go about my menial occupations for a while, keeping my new estate as secret as my princedom once had been? Then it had been a merry and delightful game, now it had become reality. (C 253)[10]

The "inventive life" realizes the dream while generating reality as a trace of the dream. What makes it become real for Krull is precisely this trace-character of reality. Such a concept of reality, such a reality effect of flirtation, simply cannot be attained with the logic of "fraud" or "deceit," terms that Krull consistently rejects as far as his "actions" are concerned. Reality or life as flirtation is not a confidence trick but rather a generating of intensities. In specifically this sense Krull is able to say that "love has no purpose, it neither wills nor thinks beyond itself . . . [it] does not think beyond a kiss at most" (C 355). Seduction is thus not an option here. It is the rhythmically appealing nothingness of the trace—in the image, in writing, in reality—which, in that it aims at "nothing at all" it initiates an intensification of life.

The generating of reality as trace/intensity is connected with a specific form of the performative, which Krull refers to as "the primeval absolute deed forever shining with newness and originality . . . *my* deed" (C 43). This is a "foray": "rapturous grab into the nearest glass urn, filled as it chanced with chocolate creams" (C 43), "free and dreamlike forays upon the sweets of life" (C 44). As an operation that carries the dream into reality, the foray also aims "at nothing" other than the generation of intensity. It is not a hunger that is satisfied but an appetite that is fed when the sweets from the delicatessen find their way to the "desk" while the trace of the dream enters into the writing utensil along with them. Yet is it a foray, a grasp, at all? Is it not much more the gesture of a grasp and/or the grasp as gesture that generates reality/life as intensity—specifically by interrupting performance in the performance?

A first foray or grasp is encountered in the opening sentence of the autobiographical notes, which begin with the words "As I take up my pen" (C 1). The first sentence in full reads:

> As I take up my pen at leisure and in complete retirement—in good
> health, by the way, though tired, so tired that I shall only be able to
> proceed by short stages and with frequent pauses for rest—as I take up
> my pen, then, to commit my confessions to this patient paper in my
> own neat and attractive handwriting, I am assailed by a brief misgiving
> about the educational back ground I bring to an intellectual enterprise
> of this kind. (C 1)[11]

Freud's "A Note upon the 'Mystic Writing-Pad' " concludes with a writing scene that transfers the rhythmic tasting of the external world by the apparatus of perception to the countermovements of two hands, of which "one hand [is] writing upon the surface of the Mystic Writing-Pad" while "another periodically raises its covering-sheet from the wax slab,"[12] on which, as Derrida notes, the "traces . . . produce the space of their inscription only by acceding to the period of their erasure."[13] Krull's *Confessions* begin with a writing scene. At issue in both texts is not what is written but rather the staging of the act of writing itself. Krull's taking up the pen has temporal dimensions that extend throughout the sentence with each dependent clause beginning "while" or "as" (*indem*). In other words the taking up of the pen *brings forth* the sentence. In this the anaphoric repetition of *indem* reveals the temporality of the grasp as that which is suspended in itself: In taking up the pen, writing is then *prepared to* write. The starting and pausing of transcription coincide in the taking up of the pen. This is not the performance of the act of writing but rather the interrupting/deferring of it in the performance of a gesture of writing, as it were, writing as a gesture, in which writing is applied back on itself. Through pausing (deferring), the taking up (the foray) becomes the pen for *tasting* writing—writing becomes a trace.

This *indem* need not only be read as "as" or "while" in the temporal sense; it also simultaneously articulates the performative dimension of the grasp/foray. *Indem* here is also *as a result of the fact that* "I take up the pen." The gesture of the grasp/the taking up of the pen not only brings forth the writing ("handwriting") in its materiality; it also initiates a rhetoric of digression. Digression and the parenthetical are the dominant rhetorical figures in the first sentence,[14] where a rhetoric of flirtation is initiated and appears here as its own artifice. Like Krull's aesthetics of existence, the aimless aim of the writing of life is also intensification, which is performed in the case of writing qua rhetorical grasps—deferral/digression—and strokes of writing (*Schriftzüge*).

The digression begins with a particle, with an adverb that is also frequently used as the story develops, *übrigens* (incidentally, by the way), prefaced by an em dash: "—übrigens gesund" (healthy, by the way). This particle begins sentences throughout the novel, up to that memorable statement uttered by the person to whom Krull is speaking in a conversation already advanced during the night train to Lisbon, "By the way: cuckoo [Übrigens: Kuckuck]" (B 304), with which he introduces himself to Krull. *Übrigens* is a recurring element in Krull's rhetoric of digression. The existence of *übrigens* has been documented since the seventeenth century as an adverb form of *übrig* (residual, left over), presumably formed under the influence of the Latin *ceterum*;[15] *übrigens* initially—and as per the meaning of *übrig*—comprises something *other* (*anderes*), something *miscellaneous* (*sonstiges*), in other words, an addition. Maass and Eberhard's *Deutsche Synonymik*, which is also cited in Grimm's *Deutsches Wörterbuch* (*German Dictionary*), defines *übrigens* as "added to what is already present"[16] and differentiates it from *ausserdem* (extra, in addition). In the case of *übrigens* what is to be added is already contained in what is present or what has been set out in the discourse,[17] while in the case of *ausserdem* it is something external to it. The meaning of *übrigens* later comes to be distinguished from that of *im übrigen* (apart from that), taking on the meaning of *nebenbei bemerkt* (incidentally noted), meaning something *beiläufig* (parenthetical, random).

It is a supplementary discourse, a discourse of supplementing, which is spun out from *übrigens* to *übrigens* and which Krull develops into the art of the digression/flirtation. The twofold meaning of *übrigens* might be instrumental in this, as the term contains both the parenthetically fleeting and the structure of the rest, the *übrig*. As the parenthetical and the rest at the same time, writing becomes intensified to become the trace, to become that rhythmically tempting nothing or *übrigens*. The written life of Felix Krull is produced through the artifice of the *übrigens*. Within the context of his autobiographical project, Krull's aesthetics of life takes on the meaning of a flirtation with writing.

Digression also characterizes Krull's writing in yet another regard. "This only by way of preface and out of its proper sequence" (C8) is only *one* self-commentary in a narrative that regularly apologizes for its "digressions" without, however, discontinuing them. In the repeated interrupting of the flow of the narrative, his digressions as well as the lack of "action" (C 79) in it that is attested to by a fictive reader, Krull's narrative strategy corresponds structurally to his rambling-desiring look into the delicatessen as well as to his "wandering" through Frankfurt. In short it is a life that neither aims at nor amounts to anything other than appetite/intensity. Thus the reader also finds himself or herself in the flirtation with Krull and therefore in a situation in which the reader should expect no "action" but rather life/reading as a trace, "exactly," according to Krull, "as though he had his own nose pressed against that pane" (C 81).

A further dimension of the art of flirtation that is already highlighted in the first sentence relates to the act of writing itself. The taking up of the pen evokes a writing scene, writing in its materiality ("in my own neat and attractive handwriting"). But in fact nothing is more questionable than the "my own" of handwriting that is claimed in this sentence, since indeed no one is more effective in disavowing this *my own* than Felix Krull himself, who never becomes tired of imitating handwriting and signatures with the greatest of precision. Tiredness, indeed disgust—as the other of the appetite—arises just that much more in the case of the signature that is ever the same: "How tiresome to sign the same name to letters and papers all one's life long! The hand grows paralyzed with irritation and disgust!" (C 50). The appetite and the tasting of writing—by means of writing—is staged, in contrast, in the structurally doubled stroke of writing that is articulated in the act of imitating. "It would interest me to see your signature" (C 249), Krull says to the Marquis de Venosta, who is shortly surprised to receive his writing from the hand of Felix Krull: " 'Incredible!' he cries. 'My writing' " (C 249). Krull's father as well would arguably—had he seen it—"have certified" Krull's perfect products of imitation "as his own" (C 32). As shown by both the delightful image of the pair of siblings on the balcony ("The beauty here lay in the duality, in the charming doubleness" [C 81]) and Krull's double flirtation with mother and daughter at the same time in Lisbon ("Mother and daughter represent the enchanting double image" [C 308]), Krull cultivates a specific affinity to the double. What is "nothing" and nonetheless "charming" is something that is structurally doubled.

What might then consequently be said about Krull is what Derrida says about the mime in "The Double Session": "He is not an imitator; he mimes imitation." The taking up of the pen initiates an order of a "supplementary double," that is, a "double that doubles no simple"; its "operation . . . alludes to nothing." This "operation, which no longer belongs to the system of truth," produces "reality-effects" nonetheless.[18] The taking up of the pen in the doubled stroke of writing brings forth Krull's life as a reality effect, indeed brings Krull himself forth as a conman. Or might the "confidence trick" not instead correspond to the doubled stroke of writing itself, which, since it does not belong to the system of truth and is therefore not "deception," would instead only be another term for "reality effect"?[19]

Krull's handwriting (*Schriftzüge*), which mimes imitation, shows the reality effect to be a "stylistic effect"[20]: In the exclusion of the signified, an absence that short-circuits the signifier and the simulated reference, it opens up a scene that, in referring back to itself, doubles itself or divides itself. Krull describes the paternal signature in "gestural writing,"[21] a description leading to a writing scene that affects itself: "The lower half of the *E* made a wide sweep to the right, in whose ample lap, so to speak, the short syllable of the last name was neatly cradled. A second flourish arose from the *u*, embracing everything before it, cutting the curve of the *E* in two places and ending in an s-shaped downstroke flanked like the curve of the *E* with ornamental rows of dots" (C 32).[22] The stroke, the "tracing of . . . writing,"[23] as the *movement* of gesture is not only described as "momentum" (*Schwung*) but also performs itself in the momentum of describing. It is the temporality of the present participle ("A second flourish arose from the *u, embracing* everything before it, *cutting* the curve of the *E* in two places and *ending* in an s-shaped downstroke") through which describing makes writing dynamic, repeating the movement of writing in gesture. In the moment of writing (in the present participle), writing is broken down into an irreducibly doubled stroke of writing/into the trace and is constituted as a relationship, as a flirtation with itself. Nothing is more real than writing's fleeting flirtation with itself in the mode of a temporality, which, as Samuel Weber's works on the present participle have shown,[24] suspends presence in the mode of being present. It is a moment that cannot be closed, a "blink of an eye"[25] that always already both precedes as well as follows itself.

In the doubled stroke of flirtation, writing and reading also come together in a relationship of reciprocal affection. The flirting reader would be one of drives and digressions, not one of confessions but one of intensities, which, according to this reading of the book, would arguably say as a result, "It was nothing, it was only charming."

THE "IRREDUCIBLY DOUBLED STROKE": FLIRTATION, FELICITY, AND SINCERITY

Lauren Shizuko Stone

Commenting on the absurdity of the pleasure that Felix Krull takes in his penmanship (as a conman and forger), Elisabeth Strowick writes, "Nothing is more questionable than the 'my own' of handwriting that is claimed in this sentence, since indeed no one is more effective in disavowing this *my own* than Felix Krull himself." In her assessment of the title figure in Mann's novel she addresses the inextricable ties among the identity (of a con man), language (in this instance writing), and the flirtatious attitude (as an aesthetic and epistemological structure); she also points us toward what I will argue is a philosophical core of flirtation: the unexpected necessity of *sincerity* in the ordinary language sense. In this essay I will examine this particular question of how Felix is constituted as Armand through language and how this con man's language *means*—where his "effective disavow[al]" situates him at the intersection of the insincere (in playfully and only temporarily adopting the identity of another) and the sincere (as the success of any con certainly depends on it being taken seriously). This tension, I will argue, is precisely what underpins flirtation; it is a kind of serious play or playful seriousness. Quite intuitively we even suspect this to be the case: To flirt effectively one has to mean it, but of course "to mean it" would mean to have unwittingly (or wittingly) shifted to the mode of seduction. In agreeing with Strowick's arguments that "Krull's aesthetics of life takes on the meaning of a flirtation" only as a project constituted in language, I would like to push the consequences of her claim a step further to suggest that in reading flirtation a deeper and much more ordinary anxiety about language per se becomes legible: that perhaps the only sincerity one can count on is the *sincerity of the one who doesn't actually mean it.*[1]

I will argue that the figure of the confidence man Felix Krull depends on a particular play in the (un)certainty in language. Crucially, this play operates at the same intersection of inner (experience) and outer (expression), which, as Wittgenstein and later Cavell have suggested, determines the way language does (or does not) capture with certainty another's experience. Because my example of flirtation is a literary one—and not necessarily an "ordinary" one—I will also use Krull to tease out a secondary claim: that literary representation offers us, generically, an insight into the nature of flirtation and that literary representation itself operates as a flirtatious object. First, I offer a brief reading of two sequential scenes of naming (when Felix "becomes" Armand) as the ambivalent identifying "operation" that, as Derrida says and Strowick has elaborated, "alludes to nothing." By describing the scene of renaming him(self) Armand as akin to Austin's transitional notion[2] of an *impure* performative—the "half descriptive, half performative" utterance—and as retained in the overlap of locutionary and illocutionary acts, Felix's flirtation as an ambivalent (speech) act as well as an epistemological and aesthetic problem becomes evident.[3] Although this first part will be a bit technical, it is precisely this question of technicality that is at work in the desire to recognize flirtation. Second, I suggest that it is despite (or because of) the inscrutability of this as an *act* that sincerity (posed initially at the level of the narrative itself) might be visible at the very heart of the flirtatious encounter.

The status of sincerity in Felix's nominal *Confessions* is already in dispute in the very first scene of putting pen to paper. As Strowick has convincingly argued, in noting the "charm" of the signature— that is, its paradoxical emptiness and doubleness—Felix both invents a double, his own and another's, and it is the former, that is *his own*, that seems to be questionably constituted. (The status of the signature as forged is not really up for debate.) And it is here that Derrida's notion of the mime is indeed an apt description. Citing Derrida, Strowick writes that it "is a 'double that doubles no simple'; its 'operation' . . . alludes to nothing.' This 'operation, which no longer belongs to the system of truth,' produces 'reality-effects' nonetheless."[4] If flirtation, as she has shown, entails both discontinuity and inventiveness, then we might want to examine precisely this operative force of naming and renaming that occurs throughout the text.

Let us as take a closer look at the scene where Felix beings his tenure as the hotel's new liftboy. Upon hiring him, the *Generaldirektor* is dissatisfied with Felix's "actual" name and flatly tells him, "Sie werden Armand genannt werden [You will be named Armand]" after the current lift boy, who, we are told, is quitting. In the following scene shortly thereafter, while riding the lift and conversing with Armand (the figure he doubles or is about to double), Felix informs him, "Ich bin nämlich jetzt Armand." (The rough translation might be "Namely, I am now Armand." More on this in a moment.)

This statement, despite its radical simplicity, provides us with the core of flirtation's appearance, specifically at the level of ordinary language. The statement "Ich bin nämlich jetzt Armand" might appear at first to be a constative—that is, merely a stating of the case. But this can hardly be simply so. Armand already works there as a lift boy, and this statement is being uttered by a narrator who claims to be Felix. Perhaps this statement might better be thought of as performative: It is outside the realm of true-false, and crucially it "does" something. The declaration inaugurates Felix *as* Armand.[5] In fact this act of mimesis (of "being Armand") could be construed as precisely his duty as lift boy. Or, in pronouncing himself to now be Armand he *becomes* Armand.

This is still not, however, what Austin calls a "pure performative" as the statement could also be argued to be half-descriptive. In saying "Ich bin nämlich jetzt Armand," Felix is describing his present condition: "To be precise, now I am Armand" (as if to say "To be precise, now I am tired" or something like this). He is being specific, as if to call attention to the possibility that there might now be *two* Armands in this elevator. But this description of what we could call a mimetic condition might itself be twofold. When we focus on the presence of this "nämlich" and include its connotation—to be fair, as an adjective instead of as adverb—it suggests another level of identity. Grammatically tenuous it is almost as if Felix is "presently the selfsame Armand." With respect to what is he the "selfsame"? With which Armand is he now identical? Recalling Strowick's arguments about how "descri[ption] makes writing dynamic," creating "an irreducibly doubled stroke," we can see that in saying "Ich bin nämlich jetzt Armand" he doubles himself, thus articulating a self-identity that lacks a stable source of initial identification.

As an impure performative it both produces a mimetic self (or, to use Austin's words, this self-production is what it "does") and also loops back on itself as a descriptive, thus producing its "reality effect" that threatens to undo any effect of reality. Felix's statement is dislodged from a true-false order and is able instead to indulge in its own suggestive force. As an essentially successful or, as Austin would say, "felicitous" use of words, the status of Felix's claim to "be" Armand reveals more than just the con man's goal: It provides an instance where the conditions of a performative utterance cannot be undermined along "procedural" lines, as the con man is already skirting the law or even writing his own laws—and, equally important, there cannot be any "infelicities" here. (To illustrate the critical difference between felicity and infelicity, compare Austin's famous example of the groom who says "I do" but is still legally married to

another woman to Felix's being "named" Armand: Although both
the still-married groom and Felix-Armand are engaging in forms of
deception, it is only the former's *act* that fails as a result; by contrast, the deception in the case of the latter is in fact necessary.) Felix's enjoyment is one of oscillation: between, on the one hand, his
new name (Armand) and, on the other hand, the ability to claim
identification with another that is completely inextricable from himself. In this way Strowick very rightly locates the legibility of the
flirtatious character in the dubious claim of "my own."

In reaction to the frequency of "impure" performatives—the fe-
licitousness of which remains unclear—Austin himself eventually revises his own terminology in favor of *acts* in language that convey
meaning (*locutionary*) or have force by convention (*illocutionary*).[6]
Even within this framework of acts, when Felix becomes Armand
through both the locution of his name and the illocution of being
named, the seriousness of such an illocutionary act remains an issue[7] since the insincerity of an utterance might still qualify as a form
of infelicity. Even under the revised conditions of illocutionary force
(over performative) the seriousness of Felix's statement "Ich bin nämlich jetzt Armand" is difficult to determine, particularly vis-à-vis any
appearance of accordance with convention (or even of philosophical logic). This also evokes the sense of both flirtation and anxiety.

This scene of naming thus vexes the idea that *meaning* (semanti-
cally) would be organized within a *practice* (what Felix "might mean"),
but the revelation of a particular conventionally constituted intention (Felix "must therefore mean X") never materializes. And it is in
this disruption or, as Strowick would say, "discontinuity," where the
figure of flirtation becomes evident. The possibility and illegibility
of any discrepancy between the *inward* intent (sincerity) of something explicitly called a confession (and with it the entire novel becomes suspect) and *outward* expression of a figure whose entire constitution is predicated on (self-)deception articulates precisely the
mode of flirtation itself: The intent of the act stands in opposition to

the outward goal (i.e., a romantic flirtation is only romantic in appearance; it must by definition intend to remain, as they say, platonic).

To get at why the inscrutability of flirtation is also a literary question I will describe the inscrutability of sincerity from another angle, and thus a short detour: In §§294–303 of the *Philosophical Investigations*,[8] Wittgenstein presents us with the idea of the "private image" (*privates Bild*)—such as a box, the contents of which we do not and cannot know—in order to try to show that despite the apparent "public," agreed-upon nature of language's descriptive properties, the connection between the inner experience of, say, the sensation of pain and its expression remains indirect at best. To do this he uses the parable of the steaming pot to get to the absurdity lurking in our use of language, by asking whether the water in the image of the pot is also boiling (§297). Here Wittgenstein impresses on his interlocutor how the conventional interpretation of another's evincing pain depends on a similar epistemological metaphor; that is, what one describes depends on the experience of one's own pain. To illustrate this he imagines two individuals, each with his own box. The other's pain corresponds, as it were, to the contents of the other's box, and the signals of pain would be the other's gesture toward the box. On Wittgenstein's view, all that one can do when faced with the outward expression of another's pain (i.e., inner experience, meaning) is assume that the contents of the other's box are *like* those in one's own. Upon closer scrutiny we see that even this "concrete" sensation becomes a cipher and quickly evades the possibility of having a "meaning." And thus the potential for the absurd also develops.

If we now consider Felix's declaration that he "is namely now Armand" the immediately registered ambivalence emphasizes the inaccessibility of what he "means" here. Though we can "understand" the words he uses, with all of the ambivalence we have already identified, we cannot verify what he *intends* by them. Felix's flirtation is thus visible precisely along these lines: We cannot know the sincerity with which he adopts the identity or name of Armand, and the

closer we inspect the mechanism of our understanding, the more absurd it becomes. For the convention of a con to be legible (as opposed to a violation of convention that would simply yield the nonsensical), the contingency between intent and expression must be
underscored. In this way, reading the indecision—the flirtation—
registered in his utterances is also a "philosophical task" that, as Cavell
notes, is "not . . . notably unlike a literary task."[9] Following Wittgenstein's reliance on the parable, Cavell writes:

> With the phrase "meaning something incoherently", I am surmising,
> and wishing to isolate . . . the possibility of meaning words in particular
> ways—e.g., ironically, parabolically, metaphorically; namely the
> possibility of meaning them all right, but of meaning them the wrong
> way, or *with an unseen sense*. Here it is the magic of words which
> returns: as if the saying of a word materialized its meaning.[10]

Felix's "invisible sincerity" coupled with a seriousness that permits
him to be both flirt and con man mirrors the inscrutability of Wittgenstein's "private image." According to Cavell, this "unseen sense"
is a way of speaking of the literary, but also what Felix *means* is not
visible to us; it thus also cannot be reduced past the two gestures I
have articulated: (1) the force of the declaration that he is *now* Armand, the illocutionary act (what Cavell calls the "magic of words"),
and (2) the locutionary act that works to convey a meaning (the literary and also the unseen). Taken together this is indeed akin to the
version of an "irreducibly doubled stroke" that Strowick has so clearly
attributed to Felix's writing.

The possibility of a flirtatious attitude, which I am attributing to
Felix (qua Armand), is conditioned on the instability in the notions
of seriousness and sincerity. Hent de Vries (in his response to Cavell)
suggests that the divide between the inward (intent, experience,
knowledge) and its outward expression is closely linked to the hilari-
ous and the absurd.[11] Rather than dismissing the absurd, it may be
helpful to embrace this side of inscrutability. On the one hand, the
Generaldirektor's hiring procedure of (re)naming Felix "Armand"—

if it is to be felicitous with respect to some convention—requires a kind of certainty coupled with seriousness on Felix's part: *certainty* insofar as Felix accepts this *as if* it were part of his job description or in fact his job title ("lift boy"), and *seriousness* in his efforts to carry out this job, assuming of course that part of its description is as it were "being Armand" (whatever that might mean). On the other hand, there is—so far as we know—no such "accepted" procedure of renaming lift boys or any other hotel employee for that matter; *eo ipso* there would be no reason to believe that Felix would, much less could, carry out such an order with anything other than insincerity. There is of course a legible form of madness in the sincerity and seriousness with which Felix, as it were, "plays" Armand (and any other roles he assumes in the novel) that would prompt us to ask the same thing de Vries does at the close of his essay on Cavell and Austin: "Are seriousness and the apparent lack thereof, like sincerity and insincerity, just two sides of the same coin, tossed up into airy space of nothingness, where no criteria are given to help us orient our ways?"[12] To the extent that Felix's declaration is simultaneously insincere and sincere—and this remains "an unseen sense" of the story line—we can no longer say that, as a flirt, he is simply "not serious" about what he does. Rather it requires that we find the necessity of *sincere deception* at the heart of the con man and the flirt alike. In this way we might look to flirtation to offer, positively, a stable form of ordinary sincerity in its insistence that *any* apparent intent was sincerely never really meant in the first place. Or, to echo Felix (and Strowick): It was nothing, only charming.

FRILL AND FLIRTATION: FEMININITY IN
THE PUBLIC SPACE

Barbara Vinken

Except for New York, which is not a typical American city, the United States in general seems to be a lousy place to flirt. One might be inclined to attribute this impression of mine to the different flirting styles that anthropologists have observed. But I don't think so. There is something deeply unflirtatious about this country: too Republican and too well Reformed; too Protestant, no irony, please! I remember arriving in the United States (New Haven, to be precise) in the mid-1980s. People in the street would never look you in the eye, let alone smile in your direction. They would simply ignore you, leave you alone and treat you as if you were invisible. If you flirted with people there, they thought that you just wanted to trick them into doing something for you or into giving you something to which you had no right.

Being flirtatious is seen as some kind of unsavory bribery you absolutely have to resist. Don't give in! Being flirtatious is just a pathetic trick for somebody who is clearly not entitled. If she were entitled, why would she go to such lengths? Why else would she rely on her charms? There was something deeply suspicious about flirting. In this frame of things, every communication is goal oriented. People inform

you, order or assist you, give or take privilege from you. They respect—
or so they probably think—your space and your independence. There
are rules for everything, no nonsense-communication that is outside
of the rules. It's the law. It was hell.

The *Oxford English Dictionary* indicates both an onomatopoetic
as well as a foreign, alien, *inevitably* French origin in the word *flirt*.
First the onomatopoetic: *Flit* means to move erratically, to flit incon-
stantly from object to object. *Flick* means to move in a jerky manner.[1] A certain lack of goal-oriented direction in this movement, a certain lack of intention can be observed. It is not clear what it is about;
it is unfocused. A lack of seriousness is perceptible, too light a touch.
The foreign, French origin is, according to some, *fleureter*, very much
like *flit*, although the notion of the flower is introduced: to touch a
thing in passing, to fly like a bee from flower to flower. According to
the *OED*, *flirt* comes from a sixteenth-century expression, *conter fleurette*. It means "to try to seduce" by dropping flower petals: to speak
sweet nothings, bagatelles.

The word itself seems strangely groundless and improper: an etymology guaranteed not in meaning but in sensuality, that is, onomatopoetic, and in the translation of a foreign word that only indicates translation, out of nothing, said metaphorically. No semantic
grounding, no proper meaning can be pinned down. Metaphor is at
the heart of flirting: to express yourself "through the flower," in another language, indirectly. And also secretly, understood only by those
in the know. For example, moles, glued onto the face, were the rage in
the eighteenth century. They were weapons in the arsenal of flirtation: One would have to be able to decipher another semiotic system. In the nineteenth century, in the wake of "oriental" fashion, they
were replaced by fans. But what precisely is to be expressed? Sheer
rhetoric, devoid of all constative qualities—the flowers—seems to be
all that there is to flirtation. And it is the origin in metaphor, an in-
between in translation, that renders flirtation void of all serious
grounding. As the *OED* puts it, "The English gallicism 'to flirt' has
made its way and has now become an anglicism." Clothes, another

metaphor for rhetoric, are part of flirting. Whereas this goes without saying for women, there also seems to be a specifically male way of flirting, namely peacocking. We'll get back to that later. But aside from translation and/or metaphor, let's keep travesty in mind. Class and gender travesties will ruin everything proper.

Serious people have always voiced an uneasiness with flirtation. Deceit, the possibility of not being taken seriously, lurks around every corner. The authenticity of our feelings is in danger. Is she or he making fun of me? The fear of being seduced, of falling prey to a show; the fear that love might be a doing rather than an essence of the innermost recesses of the heart. Flirtation is linked to wit, and wit can be devastating. *Flirt* is therefore a synonym for *coquetterie*. Being *coquette* means "to behave in a way that makes another person think you are attracted to them." To flirt is an act, and it may be a fake one: "People act amorously, often without serious intentions." You just can't tell if they mean what they say. It is impossible to decide whether they speak properly or improperly. Flirtation is a means to put off sexual intercourse indefinitely, to defer and seduce away from a finite productive result: orgasm and/or the begetting of children. It is an endless detour not directed at a fixed aim. To define flirting in a very pragmatic, utilitarian, economically successful way as "a way to meet potential mates and see (within a short period of time) whether they are compatible" seems to be off the mark. Flirting has very little to do with healthy, goal-oriented mating without much ado, no money and no time wasted. It is of another order than that of supply and demand. In terms of pop songs you could say that Michel Delpech's chanson "Pour un flirt avec toi / Je ferais n'importe quoi"[2]—*hors prix*—is just the opposite of George Harrison singing

> I got my mind set on you.
> But it's gonna take money,
> A whole lotta spending money.
> It's gonna take plenty of money
> To do it right, child.

It's gonna take time,
A whole lot of precious time . . .
To do it right, child.

Flirting, in its pleasurable, aimless, gratuitous roaming, in its sometimes devastating irony, is just the ruin of all things proper, of proper
language and proper meaning. It is a behavior that leads to the loss
of virtue, *virtus*, to the loss of manliness, *virtus* proper. It is the reign
not of the female but of effeminacy. If it were to be the reigning form
of communication, all things would be turned upside down, all values perverted.

At the dawn of the modern republics this is precisely the danger
that philosophers like Montesquieu and Rousseau foresaw in *galanterie*. And certainly flirting is essential to *galanterie*. The corrupt,
softened—that is, feminized, gallant, and we might add flirtatious—
monarchy is confronted with a manly republic, sworn to virtue, dead
serious. The republic envisages itself as an order of simplicity and
rigor. Along with equality and fraternity, it proclaims the necessity
for the feminine to disappear from the public sphere. Monarchy is
denounced as a political form, a public space, given entirely over to
galanterie. For the sake of argument, we might say, with a slight anachronism: Monarchy was seen as a society where flirtation was the dominant form of communication. And with flirtation, women reigned.
To put it another way: It was a process whereby man proper, *virtus*,
was trapped in a constant process of corruption and decay. At least
this is how Montesquieu and Rousseau saw it. Proper meaning, proper
sexuality was perverted. The space where the sexes mingled instead
of being separated—the court or salon versus the public space and the
home—results in the end of male *virtus* and female modesty.

In a mixed society, where the private and the public, the home and
politics, were not separated and where therefore the sexes mixed,
galanterie, the trifles that turned everything into nothingness, reigned
supreme. It was women, with their minds only on bagatelles, who
were seen as the agent of corruption. As Montesquieu elegantly puts it:

The society of women spoils mores and forms taste; the desire to please more than others establishes ornamentation, and the desire to please more than oneself establishes fashions. Fashions are an important subject; as one allows one's spirits to become frivolous, one constantly increases the branches of commerce.[3]

In monarchies women have so little restraint because, called to court by the distinction of ranks, they there take up the spirit of liberty that is almost the only one tolerated. Each man uses their charms and their passions to advance his fortune; and as their weakness allows them not arrogance but vanity, luxury always reigns there with them.[4]

With women, idleness, luxury, *galanterie*, and *libertinage* reign. Their domain is one of sweet nothingness. Men are forced to submit to an empty arbitrary tyranny, in order to avoid being judged ridiculous. All values are turned upside down; nothingness becomes everything.

In such a society, exclusively determined by appearance and spectacle, catastrophe cannot be far away. The difference of the sexes threatens to be erased, manliness corrupted. The desire of the women to please and that of men to please them, in turn, leads to both sexes losing their essential properties. It may be ridiculous when women become men, but it is horrifying to see men turn into women. Rousseau sees this perversion in the Babel that cities have become, where the public influence of women has turned men into slaves in a kind of seraglio dominated by women. "Unable to make themselves into men, the women make us into women," declares Rousseau.[5] A political discourse will henceforth no longer be separable from a discourse on gender and on flirtation, *galanterie*. A particular social class of men, nobility, and a particular form of sovereignty, monarchy, are characterized by a lack of masculinity. In a monarchy men have to disguise themselves as women. This sickness spreads like a plague. It threatens the pure, free, republican, and, not least, Calvinist Geneva. "On my last trip to Geneva, I already saw several of these young *ladies* in jerkins"—Rousseau is describing young men here, and jerkins is a *just au corps*, a very tight-fitting jacket that, contrary to the bourgeois loose-fitting jacket, models the body tightly through tailoring—"with white teeth, plump hands, piping voices, and pretty green parasols in their hands, rather maladroitly counterfeiting men."[6] This image of a seraglio, like the sultan's court, inhabited by eunuchs and ruled over by flirting women with frills on their dresses, moving nothing but their tongues to talk about trifles, thus becomes the very opposite of the antique, pure, Spartan republic.[7] Republicans don't flirt.

In the age of Consumer Culture, has flirtation become a commodity, a service to sell, a means to sell? Up to a certain point, yes. Doormen, waitresses, vendors may not be expected to flirt, but certainly to compliment, to flatter, to coax, to seduce, in what might be the remnants of a culture of gallantry. The woman, the young girl, has turned flirtation into a commodity of femininity and femininity into a commodity.[8]

But, then again, perhaps not. Who flirts today? Serious businessmen? No; if anything, they perhaps harass. Women? Since they are no longer the weaker sex but instead the moral sex, not really. At least not when they, under the spell of a certain feminism, have become so serious as to leave behind all vanity, frills, trifles, and irony. Flirtation, if not commodified, has become an activity on the margins. It is a way of coping with not being taken seriously by asserting that seriousness is not an option. By showing dead seriously that deadly seriousness is but a masquerade—to be taken seriously.

The gentlemen of Bacongo, peacocking, come to mind. Frills are their life. Peacocking, you might recall, is a male or maybe not so male way to flirt. So let's look at some men who are clearly the new women. And who, through sheer mimicry, will make real men, white middle-class men, look awkward. They turn the self-effacing parade of male power into a masquerade.[9] Here again we have a translation: The object of colonization dresses as its master-subject once did. I am talking about the "gentlemen of Bacongo," beautifully photographed by Daniele Tamagni, with an introduction by that contemporary dandy Paul Smith.[10]

Images are taken from Daniele Tamagni, *Gentlemen of Bacongo* (London: Trolley Books, 2009), no pagination. Copyright: Daniele Tamagni. I would like to thank Daniele Tamagni for his generous permission.

I ran into these *sapeurs* in real life in Paris, in the vicinity of the metro station Château d'Eau. And then a second time in a novel by Alain Mabanckou, *Black Bazaar*. I learned that these gentlemen from Bacongo live in a swinging diaspora in Paris and Brussels and that they are members of SAPE: Société des Ambianceurs et des Personnes Élégantes. As a member of this most exclusive of all exclusive clubs, Mabanckou's hero never buys from the rack but wears only Savile Row.

> I am always wearing a suit to keep up the pressure, as we say back home among the SAPE, Société des Ambianceurs et des Personnes Élégantes. This scene was invented, although many dispute this, in the quarter of Bacongo in Brazzaville, close to the roundabout by the TOTAL market. It was us who exported the SAPE to Paris, and that's sheer fact. Despite all the false, self-proclaimed prophets roaming the streets of the city of love who make it difficult to separate fact from fiction.[11]

These "dressmen" live with six people in one room and earn the little money they do by the sweat of their brow. But Mabanckou's hero owns as many suitcases of bespoke suits and crocodile-leather Westons as any diva would. He pursues the most feminine activity: He shops until he drops. What to wear is the only question our hero takes seriously. A dandy, as the famous definition in Carlyle's *Sartor Resartus* goes, is a clothes-wearing man.[12] While others dress to live, he lives to dress. To dress is his job. A peacock, he loves to be adored for his incredible elegance, his very *raison d'être*.

> I couldn't make up my mind which suit to wear. I had opened all the suitcases, all my things were scattered on the floor and on the bed. I finally decided on a bottlegreen suit by YVES SAINT LAURENT, with bordeaux Westons. Even our Arab from around the corner came out of his shop, when he smelt my perfume. . . . But why not delight in the stares of the bypassers? . . . I rearranged my knot and smoothed my pants so that they fell beautifully over my shoes. I opened three buttons of my jacket, a little trick so that people could marvel at my Christian Dior belt.[13]

The *sapeurs* put all their energy into the high art of detail: how to knot a tie properly, how to choose the perfect socks: "Tell me how you knot your tie and I will tell you who you are." It doesn't matter what you wear, it's how you wear it: This dandyesque maxim is still that of the modern *sapeurs*. Style is everything.[14] The *sapeur*, a colonized subject that cross-dresses, puts on a travesty of class and race.[15] By putting on a suit, uniform of the white man, the *sapeur* resists all kinds of identity politics. It was, after all, the president of Congo, Mobutu Sese Seko, who in 1971 banned the dress of the colonizer, suit and tie, for the authentic, African clothes. The *sapeur* wears precisely that: the uniform of the bourgeois, white colonizer. Only better. This theatricalization of the body put ostentatiously on display is within the bourgeois white order the burden or privilege of the female sex alone. By doing this, men become effeminate and ruin all maleness proper. The *sapeur* does it all: He travesties sex, class, and race—in a wink, with a frill.

The verb *saper* is not only an argot word for being dressed, as in *bien ou mal sapé*. The *sapeurs* are an elite unit of the French Army; these *sapeurs* "sap" in the sense of hollowing out the foundations of buildings prior to their destruction, their work quite literally that of "undermining." The *sapeurs* from Congo bring down the reigning order of sex, class, and race, seen as the most natural thing in the world, through an ostentatious mimicry. In the ruins left, "the empire writes back." By cross-dressing with an iron will-to-style and against all odds as the colonial lord, as the bourgeois gentlemen, these "eccentric" people in Tamagni's shots become postmodern heroes. They put the master back on stage as spectacular debris. The gentleman, clad in pink from hat to toe, Cohiba between his teeth, comes straight at us on the cover of Tamagni's photoreportage. He is a flirt.

LEARNING TO FLIRT WITH DON JUAN

Christophe Koné

My experience of flirtation in America differs significantly from that of Barbara Vinken; the United States has a very flirtatious culture. I cannot count the numerous times when I was approached by perfect strangers who commented on my appearance, approved of my outfits, shared their unsolicited opinion about my style, or simply inquired about the provenance of my clothes. Whether in urban centers, suburban or rural areas, in the street, on the train, or in a store, you cannot keep strangers from approaching you! Flirtatious interjections punctuate your daily life in the United States, and you rarely can run away from an enthusiastic "I love your X!"—not to mention the various "My Dears," "Honeys," and "Sweethearts" immediately thrown at you from the moment you come into contact with a medical assistant or a sales associate.

Although such interactions strengthen the social fabric and oil the wheels of consumer culture by facilitating the exchange of information about service and consumer goods, they are far from being exhausted by this function: With "Sweetheart" or "I love your X!," the possibility of flirtation cannot be excluded. (Nor can the possibility of harassment be excluded either.) Whether the recipient reacts to these phrases with amusement or irritation, they nevertheless leave him or her bewildered because unsure about where to stand and where to go from there. Flirtation is by definition neither a sincere nor a serious act; it is casual, even superficial, and fundamentally playful, which is the reason why flirting can be deceitful.[1] Since flirtation always keeps things in play, the fear of misunderstanding the rules of the game or simply not playing by the rules always lurks. If flirting is all about play and fun, the game is fun as long as you are neither being "played" nor being made fun of. Playfulness and amusement are part of the definition of *flirt*. According to the new *Oxford Dictionary*, *to flirt* means "to behave as though attracted to or trying to attract someone, but for amusement rather than with serious intentions," while the *Merriam-Webster Dictionary* has "to behave in a way that shows a sexual attraction for someone but is not meant to be taken seriously." What both definitions have in common is their emphasis on a complete lack of seriousness, as well as the contrast between appearance and intent.

In her essay "Frill and Flirtation," Vinken shows us that even the "unfocused" etymology of the word *flirt*, with its supposedly French origin, seems to perform, as it were, a certain "lack of seriousness." Vinken links *flirt* with the verb *fleureter*, "to fly like a bee from flower to flower," and the idiom *conter fleurette*, "dropping flower petals: to speak sweet nothings, bagatelles." In the movement from one flower to the next and in the speaking of "sweet nothings," the unlikely image of Don Juan also appears. Although the title figure imagined by Molière in his 1665 play, *Don Juan or the Feast with the Statue*, is typically associated with *seduction* rather than flirtation, the movement of the serial philanderer and his acting skills point to precisely this intertwining of noncommitment and performance. Throughout Molière's play Don Juan flies like a bee from woman to woman and tells sweet nothings to many a protagonist, male and female alike, to get his way. The servant Sganarelle, in a conversation with Don Juan in Act I, scene 2, depicts his master's fickle conduct in the following terms: "Your heart is the greatest nomad that ever was. It likes

to be always on the move. It hates to stay in one place for long together."[2] Although this literary character has been regarded by scholars mainly as a seducer, I would like to offer a different reading of
Don Juan and argue that he is, in fact, quite a flirt and that we can
learn a great deal from him about flirting![3]

In his first appearance onstage at the beginning of the first act,
Don Juan in a long soliloquy expresses not only his scornful disbe-
lief in faithfulness ("Constancy is only fit for idiots") but also his self-
identification with a belligerent warrior who unbeatably collects con-
quests and victories one after the other:

> There is nothing so sweet as to overcome the resistance of a beautiful
> woman; and, where they are concerned, I have the ambition of a
> conqueror, who goes from triumph to triumph, and can never be
> satisfied. Nothing shall stand in the way of my desire. My heart is big
> enough to love the whole world; and I could wish with Alexander, that
> there were more worlds still, so that I might carry yet further my
> prowess in love.[4]

The restlessness of Don Juan's floating desire—an inability to stay put—
links the philanderer to the flirt. According to the *Merriam-Webster*
dictionary, *to flirt* is related to *flit* and *flick* and also means "to move
erratically," and thus gestures toward the deeply rooted idea of aimless and restless movement in the notion of flirtation. And yet, for
all its erratic movements in space, going from one object to the next,
flirtation never steps out of line. In other words, flirtation walks the
line of seduction without ever crossing it. Flirtation overtly flirts with
seduction; after all, they both use (spoken and body) language as a
tool to achieve their goal, and yet their respective goals are precisely
what set them apart from one another. Unlike seduction, flirting does
not go all the way but rather remains safely at the margins and on
the edge; hence the idiom "flirting with disaster," in the sense of coming close to disaster but never quite coming into contact with it.

Molière's Don Juan flirts in all senses of the word: Not only does
he wander purposelessly through various places in Sicily (from a

palace, a country place by the sea, a forest, his own apartment, to a place in the country near the city), but he also flirts with characters of both genders and from various social classes, such as the peasants Charlotte and Mathurine and the bourgeois shopkeeper M. Dimanche. And he also flirts with disaster throughout the play, until he crosses the line in his encounter with the statue of the commander and thereby brings about his own demise. The deathly statue ultimately intervenes to put an end to flirtation and the arch-flirt Don Juan; Don Juan will flirt with disaster no more.

Oddly enough, among all the characters of Molière's comedy, the only one with whom Don Juan does not flirt is his noble wife, Dona Elvira. She is in fact seduced, in the literal and figurative senses: She is persuaded to disobey (she left a cloister to follow Don Juan); she is led astray by false promises (he married her and left her alone) and enticed into sexual intercourse (she lost her virginity to him). In Act I, scene 3, the dignified Dona Elvira, repudiated and offended, comes to town to confront Don Juan, just to realize too late that she has fallen victim to a seducer. Pretending to be plagued with religious scruples, when in fact he abandoned his wife to pursue a new love interest, Don Juan gives her the following justification:

> I have mediated on the fact that, in order to marry you, I stole you from
> the cloister; that you have broken vows which committed you to
> another life, and that Heaven is a jealous rival. Fearful of divine wrath,
> I have repented my sin. I have recognized that our marriage was nothing
> but adultery in disguise, which would bring on us some dreadful
> punishment; and that it was my duty to try to forget you, and allow you
> to return to your lawful obligations.[5]

It is also worth emphasizing that Dona Elvira's seduction was a plan Don Juan purposely carried out: He did not flirt with her but courted her according to her high rank, seduced her, and ultimately married her. This is what her equerry Gusman recalls when, in conversation with Don Juan's servant Sganarelle at the very beginning of the play, he shares his bewilderment: "I cannot understand how, after all the love and impetuosity he has shown, the homage, the vows, the sighs, the tears, the passionate letters, the protestations, the oft-repeated oaths, his savage determination in forcing even the scared doors of a convent to gain possession of Dona Elvira; how, after all that, he can have the heart to go back on his word."[6] Dona Elvira's noble origin as well as her seduction set her apart from the other characters of lesser rank with whom Don Juan flirts shamelessly. The difference, though, between her and the others, I would argue, lies in her capacity to use language skillfully. Unlike the peasant girls and the bourgeois shopkeeper, Dona Elvira does not misunderstand Don Juan's language; her parody of him at the end of the first act demonstrates that she can also speak the language of seduction. As her example suggests, seduction is at odds with flirtation since it is a serious matter that carries consequences and does not lend itself to the comic. Dona Elvira, the outraged woman, stands as the tragic character in the play, and this explains why she leaves the stage with a warning addressed to Don Juan: "I say again, Heaven will punish you, you faithless villain; and if you are not afraid of Heaven, at least beware the anger of the wife you have betrayed."[7]

The beginning of the second act of *Don Juan* shows the title figure caught in the act of flirting with peasant girls. After his plan to abduct a young fiancée at sea fails and ends in shipwreck, Don Juan, on the rebound, catches sight of a peasant girl named Charlotte, with whom he immediately starts flirting. Approaching her in the company of his male servant Sganarelle, he exclaims, "What a ravishing creature! What sparkling eyes! . . . Was ever anything more delightful? . . . What a pretty figure! . . . Oh, what a delicate little face! Let me look right into your eyes. How beautiful! Will you allow me to see your teeth? Oh, they are made for love. And these tempting lips as well. I am quite enchanted. I have never seen so charming a person."[8] The fortuitous encounter between a flirtatious nobleman and a peasant girl is a key scene in many aspects: Not only does it validate the definition of flirtation previously given, but it also foregrounds the significant part that language plays in the act of flirting. The spectator, already in the know, appreciates and enjoys the comic situation of the scene at the expense of the peasant girl. The naïve Charlotte ends up being an object of ridicule because she misreads Don Juan's deceitful behavior and misunderstands his insincere speech, particularly when he tells her sweet nothings such as "I speak from the very bottom of my heart" and "I love you, fair Charlotte, with all my heart."[9] Since the ignorant girl does not play by the rules of flirtation—that is, she takes Don Juan's words at face value—she is ultimately played by the skilled flirter for the spectator's amusement. By relying on the social and educational disparities between the two characters, this scene demonstrates that flirting operates at the level of performance and language and is further grounded in misunderstanding. The flirt Don Juan, endowed with a silver tongue, is at the top of his game, whereas the tongue-tied Charlotte cannot keep up. "I am too simple to know how to answer," she replies, then adds, "I've heard that you court folk are all *dissemblers*."[10]

This structure repeats itself in Act IV with Don Juan in his flirtatious encounter (as both a showman and a dissembler) with a shopkeeper named M. Dimanche. Here the flirt displays such tactical mastery of language that the bourgeois creditor, who pays him a visit to collect his money, takes his leave without ever claiming his due. At the sight of M. Dimanche, Don Juan overwhelms the shopkeeper with a flow of flirtatious talk—"I hope I see you well, Monsieur Dimanche. . . . You have a regular fund of good health; full lips, fresh colour, and bright eyes"—before bidding him farewell: "Embrace me Monsieur Dimanche. And, once more, I beg you to believe that I am entirely at your service. There is nothing in the world I would not do for you."[11] It is worth observing the similarity between the scene with M. Dimanche and the previous one with Charlotte since Don Juan uses a similar tactic in both: He praises his interlocutors' physical appearance (the beauty of the peasant girl and the vigor of the shopkeeper), but he does so for the spectator's entertainment, and thus ultimately at the expense of these foolish characters.

Throughout the play Don Juan takes great pleasure in the linguistic performance of flirtation. Molière's maxim of comic flirtation would seem to be: He who in his speech can walk the line of seduction without crossing it will have a lot of fun in flirtation, whereas he who cannot read between the lines of flirtatious talk will be made fun of. Focusing on Don Juan's series of broken promises as well as their linguistic implications in the play, Shoshana Felman in *The Literary Speech Act* points out the following: "The desire of a Don Juan is thus at once desire for desire and desire for language; a desire that desires itself and that desires its own language. Speech is the true realm of eroticism, and not simply a means to access this realm."[12]

An anterior scene depicts Don Juan caught in his own flirting game and now entangled with two peasant girls quarrelling over which one will be his promised. Pressed by both Charlotte and Mathurine to tell the truth, a vexed Don Juan answers, "Argument leads nowhere. It's deeds that count, not words," before resuming his alternating flirtation with the two girls: "[aside to Mathurine] I adore you. [aside to Charlotte] I am yours forever. [aside to Mathurine] All other faces are ugly besides yours. [aside to Charlotte] It would be impossible to love anyone else after you."[13] Reading Molière's *Don Juan* through the lens of Austin's speech act theory, Felman observes, "What is really at stake in the play—the real conflict—is, in fact, the opposition between two views of language, one that is cognitive, or constative, and another that is performative."[14] Unlike his victims and pursuers in the comedy, who view language as a vessel of truth and knowledge, "language, for Don Juan is performative and not informative; it is a field of enjoyment, not of knowledge."[15]

Although Felman does not differentiate between seduction and flirtation in her analysis of Molière's comedy (and therefore regards its main protagonist primarily as a seducer), her examination is nevertheless instrumental to my reading of him as a flirt. I would like to nuance Felman's interpretation, since Molière's play presents a few instances where Don Juan's seductive power is not quite yet in full swing but within which his flirtation is on full display, as in his

interactions with Charlotte, Mathurine, and M. Dimanche. If the id-
iosyncrasy of Don Juan as seducer, according to Felman, lies in his
misuse or abuse of performative speech in the form of (unkept)
promises with which he always gets away (and gets *his way*), then I
would advance that Don Juan as flirt performs the very conflict of
the play, that is, the antagonism between constative and performative speech acts. In fact while flirting with either peasant girls or a
bourgeois shopkeeper, the main protagonist navigates the tension
between both, since flirting walks the line between constative and
performative. The flirtatious utterances Don Juan addresses to Charlotte, such as "What a ravishing creature! What sparkling eyes! . . .
What a pretty figure! . . . Oh, what a delicate little face!," speak the
truth of his erotic desire for her, and yet this spoken desire is anything but binding: It remains uncommitted and does not seek any
completion at all. In that respect, flirtation is the opposite of performative even though the flirt is quite a performer. Put slightly differently, the constitutive possibility of failure in the performative of seduction pushes this speech act toward a flirtatious zone. With a nod
to Nietzsche, we might characterize it as "beyond success and failure." As Molière's Don Juan demonstrates, flirtation thus comes not
with a promise but with a prospect.

FLIRTATION AND TRANSGRESSION

INTERLUDE

THREE TERRORS OF FLIRTATION

Barbara Natalie Nagel

Nothing seems more harmless than a flirt. But then why at times the feeling of sheer terror? Why do people turn pale and flee? "Hans Castorp was excited about the encounter, at the same time he felt something like ascending anxiety, a trepidation of the same kind as being confined with the happenstance someone in narrow space caused in him."[1] Thomas Mann is one of those authors all too familiar with the terrors of flirtation, including the risk of ridicule. And according to one scientific study, the effect of flirtation is nothing short of alarming: "The moment of attraction, in fact, mimics a kind of brain damage."[2] Feelings of stress, nervousness, and panic are accompanied by rising blood pressure and cold sweat.

In many scenes of flirtation we experience an almost sadistic pleasure in witnessing the crack-up of authority figures (even if it is Mann's antihero Hans Castorp). While these moments are usually interpreted as mere reversals of master-slave dialectics, it is rather the potential destabilization of the power structure as a whole—including, but not limited to, the male—that is experienced as traumatic. Nothing is more threatening than the suspension of authority, if only for a moment.

It is precisely this suspension, however, that flirtation triggers because
it does not show the same infatuation with authority that dominates
the discourse of seduction.

If we look more closely at what happens in flirtation, then the terror of flirtation results from at least three sources. First, the epistemological shock: "Are we flirting?" Or maybe worse: "Is he/she just a
flirt?" Very poignantly Henry James's famous story about "a pretty
American flirt,"[3] *Daisy Miller*, bears the subtitle *A Study*. For we never
just flirt—rather we study our object, we observe it, and lose ourselves
in this observation: "He thought it very possible that [Miss Daisy] was
a coquette; he was sure she had a spirit of her own; but in her bright,
sweet, superficial little visage there was no mockery, no irony."[4] In
this way flirtation brings up the impossible question of sincerity;
James's perplexed narrator is "reduced to chopping logic about this
young lady."[5] If ever we are to gain certainty about the status of the
flirtation it is because the flirtation is over—and we, in the meantime,
have moved into another state.

The second source of terror arises from the sudden, queer inversion, or in-betweenness of power in flirtation. An inversion often
coincides with an inversion of gender roles occurring in heterosex-
ually structured scenes of flirtation: "In saying no and saying yes, in
surrendering and refusing to surrender themselves, women are the
masters,"[6] Georg Simmel marvels. Simmel's object of study is European women at the beginning of the twentieth century who in flirtation experience a rare "fascination of freedom and power," that is,
a fascination of which they are normally deprived. This female em-
powerment is the result of a queer role switch: The woman "takes
on his decision, even if only in a symbolic and approximate fashion."[7]
To some twentieth-century men this role switch can be quite unset-
tling. Maybe that is the reason a philosopher like Sartre, in his brief
writing on flirtation, hastily dismisses the idea of feminine sovereignty
as mere erotic cluelessness on the woman's part:

> Take the example of a woman who has consented to go out with a
> particular man for the first time. She knows very well his intentions. . . .

> She knows also that it will be necessary sooner or later for her to make
> a decision. But she does not want to realize the urgency. . . . If he says
> to her, "I find you so attractive!" she disarms this phrase of its sexual
> background. . . . This is because she does not quite know what she
> wants.[8]

What Sartre loses sight of here are the aspects of freedom and play.
Instead he demands woman's immediate submission to the coital teleology, a purpose for which he mobilizes the Hegelian concept of
bad faith (*Unaufrichtigkeit*) and makes it his own (*mauvaise foi*, "a
lie to oneself"),[9] as if the female flirt would willfully lack conscience.
For Sartre a decision about sex or no-sex must be made instanta-
neously; otherwise the woman in the café is wasting everybody's time.
But according to Simmel something quite different is at stake in the
heterosexual scene of flirtation: Women don't prolong the flirtation
because they aren't aware of their own desire but because, on the
contrary, they intend to enjoy their freedom for as long as possible.

But how long is "as long as possible"? Sartre's impatience is an effect of the third terror of flirtation: Where seduction is not possible
any longer because no one gains the upper hand, because no one
surrenders, flirtation becomes endless. In 2013 an ad on New York
Craigslist's Missed Connection section went viral; the ad begins as
these kinds of ads tend to begin: "I saw you on the Manhattan-bound
Brooklyn Q train. I was wearing a blue-striped t-shirt and a pair of
maroon pants. You were wearing a vintage red skirt and a smart white
blouse. We both wore glasses. I guess we still do."[10] But then the text
drags on for no fewer than seventy-seven lines, which equal an infinite number of subway rides, which equal sixty years of quiet eye
contact; the flirtatious subway ride is stuck in a Möbius strip because
the flirtation refuses to take off to something else, until one person
finally leaves the train:

> One day, in the middle of the afternoon, you stood up as the train
> pulled into Queensboro Plaza. It was difficult for you, this simple task of
> standing up, you hadn't done it in sixty years. Holding onto the rails,
> you managed to get yourself to the door. You hesitated briefly there,

perhaps waiting for me to say something, giving me one last chance to
stop you, but rather than spit out a lifetime of suppressed almost-
conversations I said nothing, and I watched you slip out between the
closing sliding doors.

The constellation depicted in the Craigslist ad shows that one of the
factors that can make flirtation an infinite process is a temporary
equality between the agents of flirtation. The source of this equality, however, remains one of flirtation's enigmas: Does flirtation happen only between people who are equal in status? Or does flirtation
equalize people? That is, while we are flirting, can we ever *not* regard each other as queer equals?

A number of the most exquisite scenes of flirtation in literature
and the visual arts are indeed staged between equals, often in ho-
mosocial constellations. Take Heinrich von Kleist's deadly flirtation
between Achilles and the Amazon queen Penthesilea; take the erotic
struggles between two brothers in Jean Genet's and later Rainer Werner Fassbinder's *Querelle de Brest*; or look at Francis Bacon's *Wres-
tlers*: It is here that flirtation unleashes an entropic terror caused by
the ostensible parity that characterizes the flirtation; it is here that
one can witness what it might mean for flirtation to be an infinite,
aimless endeavor. In a constellation of (approximate and however vol-
atile) parity, flirtation must end in utter exhaustion or death. Flirtation hence comes close to what Jean-François Lyotard calls "sterile

pleasure"—a form of *jouissance*, of intense enjoyment, of pleasure that serves no purpose and in this frivolous purposivelessness resembles a child watching a match burn down: "But when a child strikes the matchhead *to see* what happens—just for the fun of it—he enjoys the movement itself, the changing colors, the light flashing at the height of the blaze, the death of the tiny piece of wood, the hissing of the tiny flame. He enjoys these sterile differences leading nowhere, these uncompensated losses; what the physicist calls the dissipation of energy."[11]

THE LUXURY OF SELF-DESTRUCTION: FLIRTING WITH MIMESIS WITH ROGER CAILLOIS

John Hamilton

In 1915, at the urging of the editors of the psychoanalytic journal *Imago*, Freud composed "Timely Thoughts on War and Death," in which he offers some reflections on the failures of enlightened civilization and the consequent change in general attitudes toward death. Whereas before this devastating war it might have been possible to evade any serious consideration of our own passing away—to "shelve" death for another day, to postpone it into the vague future—today, in 1915, given the massive scope and cruelty of the Great War, we are compelled to face death head-on: "Death can no longer be denied; one must believe in it."[1] Death is now making unequivocal advances, demanding attention and refusing to be ignored. One might surmise that the ubiquity and hence inescapability of death would have a debilitating effect on the psyche, plunging it into the listless indifference of melancholia. Yet, as Freud goes on to argue, the present undeniable nature of death is hardly detrimental. On the contrary, it allows life to become significant again for the very reason that its mortality is fully acknowledged. Certainly experiencing death vividly entails the stark recognition of one's own possible demise,

which can arrive at any moment. Yet by being conscious of this im-
minence one gains the sense of still being alive, a confirmation of
having survived. Taking life seriously grants us an occasion to take
life itself seriously, in all its fragility and contingency. We thereby ap-
preciate the fact that our life has been preserved, at least for now. In
denying death, in shunting it off indefinitely for later consideration,
we would rob ourselves of the opportunity to believe in self-
preservation.

In Freud's view, prior to the great disenchantment triggered by
the war and its unheard-of casualties, the ego did not truly believe
in its own death and therefore did not believe in its own life:

> Life is impoverished, it loses its interest, when the highest stake in the
> game of living, precisely life itself, should not be risked. It becomes as
> vapid, as inane as an American flirtation [*Es wird so schal, gehaltlos wie
> etwa ein amerikanischer Flirt*], in which it is from the first determined,
> that nothing is going to happen, in contrast to a continental love affair
> in which both partners must constantly bear in mind the serious
> consequences. (343)

Leaving aside the off-hand cultural critique that contrasts American
levitas with European *gravitas*, I would like to focus on this quick
characterization of flirtation in relation to the topics of self-
preservation, representation, and mimesis. For Freud, back when Eu-
ropeans could still afford to be insipid, the common way to imagine
one's own unimaginable demise was by means of representation. In-
capable of believing in one's own mortality, one essentially "flirted"
with death by being the spectator of another's death—an aesthetic
device for framing and thereby representing the unrepresentable without any "serious consequences." Our own end—our mortal *telos*—
could be suspended in this aestheticizing gesture. However now, in
1915, when the possibility of death has become undeniable, when
we "must believe in it," when the *end* is in sight, the evasive, non-
committal gestures of the flirt are no longer viable. Instead the adult
stakes of an adulterous relationship with death become clarified: The

death of the other spells one's own mortality. Carefree attitudes of immortality have been replaced by a solicitous consideration of contingent survival. Through mourning we come to realize our own preservation; we are given concrete proof that we have been spared, at least for now.

Freud's portrayal of flirtation as "vapid" and "inane" (*schal und gehaltlos*) comes very close to a typically Platonic view of mimesis as an activity that produces merely inessential copies. From this perspective resemblance is strictly distinguished from the model. For Freud the mimetic image afforded by the death of another used to work as a strategy of psychic defense insofar as the idea of mimesis generally operates by way of a dissimilar similarity. It offered an image that corresponds to the observing consciousness, inviting identification with the reflection, while spoiling, again through reflection, any complete identification. In framing the death of the other, the image literally made death *imaginable*: a picture that corresponded to the subject's possible destruction while marking enough difference to affirm the unconscious belief in one's immortality. In confronting this contained, comprehensive picture we were able to blow death off like an American flirt, to flick it away with a sudden release of the fingernail from the thumb, which appears to be the onomatopoetic source of the Anglicism *flirt*. Just as the flirt imitates the serious lover, so the serious implications of one's own annihilation can be flirted away by means of imitation. In contrast, now compelled to "believe" in the image—now forced to acknowledge that the image of death is no image at all but rather something that directly pertains to our own fragile existence—this encounter brutally disrupts the comfortable distance once afforded by the similar yet dissimilar image. Our engagement with the other can no longer be taken so lightly.

For Freud life is as vapid and inane as an American flirtation when it traffics in merely imitative images. Flirtation simply mimics serious advances and therefore establishes a psychic zone of safety, where the unconscious suffers no impingements that might upset its denial of death. Yet what if mimesis itself were not such an easy game to

play? What if the distinction between correspondence and all-out identification were not so simple to maintain? What if the apotropaic gesture of flicking something off concealed a more profound fear? Does
flirtation, in its presumably nonserious play with matters of real consequence, in fact harbor something that is perfectly threatening?

Freud's view is congruent with a Platonic tradition that decidedly
attempts to weaken the allure of mimesis by reducing it to a subor-
dinate, inessential function. In order to do so it consistently underscores the dissimilarity that distinguishes the resemblance from the
thing resembled. Accordingly it expresses concern over the possible
erasure of difference that nonetheless remains latent in mimetic affairs. Socrates, for example, ridicules Cratylus for taking mimesis to
denote the production of a perfect similarity unmarred by difference.
To this end he offers a conjectured scenario:

> An image [*eikōn*] cannot remain an image if it presents all the details of
> what it represents. See if I'm right. Would there be two things—Cratylus
> and an image of Cratylus [*Kratylou eikōn*]—in the following circum-
> stances? Suppose some god didn't just represent your color and shape
> the way painters do, but made all the inner parts like yours, with the
> same warmth and softness, and put motion, soul, and wisdom like
> yours into them—in a word, suppose he made a duplicate of everything
> you have and put it beside you. Would there then be two Cratyluses or
> Cratylus and an image of Cratylus?[2]

Socrates broaches the possible but improbable case of creating a perfectly identical image of his interlocutor, one that a god has endowed
with every particular physical, emotional, and rational attribute.
Should such a creation be feasible, Socrates suggests, we would no
longer be dealing with an image at all but rather with an exact, indistinguishable duplication. As the reduplicated form of the word
mimēsis itself suggests—and as Cratylus should notice—the split
between the first and second phonemes, *mi* and *mē*, marks a difference held together by similarity. According to Socrates, Cratylus
is "ridiculous" because he fails to recognize that the postulate of

correspondence must include a certain measure of dissimilarity. The philosopher tries to scare his friend straight by conjuring not a playful image but a true *Doppelgänger*, a figure that can effectively and seriously undercut the foundation of a singular, nonexchangeable subject.

All the same, Socrates' argument barely conceals a certain risk. Despite the absurdity of his example, mimesis remains a real threat insofar as it flirts with complete identity, including the notion of a singular, indivisible, unrepeatable individuality. In the extreme case of absolute similarity—a case to which Cratylus's argument ultimately must lead—there would be no more difference, no more distinctions, which are necessary for preserving the stability of personal identity. This threat of mimesis is nowhere more pronounced than in Plato's *Republic*, where the guardians must be shielded from the seduction of poetry, from the way poetry comes on strong, inducing its listener to become someone else. The guardians might lose their capacity to protect the city should they be lured into identifying with the representation. They might become weak or impotent, fearful or irresolute. In a word: They might become feminized. He who plays the coward might become one. "Imitations practiced from youth become part of nature and settle into habits of gesture, voice, and thought."[3] Beware, Socrates seems to warn, lest you become the mask you're wearing!

Mimesis may only flirt with identity, but this flirtation continues to threaten our individual, social, and political relationships. Noteworthy is the first example that Socrates offers in order to demonstrate the danger of mimesis, namely the story from Hesiod's *Theogony*, in which Kronos castrates his father, Ouranos.[4] On the one hand, Socrates would appear to be justified in censoring such stories about the gods, which would clearly establish an insidious precedent for seditious behavior among the citizenry. On the other hand, and of particular interest here, is that the very thought of mimesis seems capable of conjuring images of disempowerment and the violent destruction of virility, of parricide and regicide. Face-to-face with mimesis, both the sovereignty of the subject and the subjectivity of the sovereign appear to be at risk, exposed to utter dismantling. For a philosopher of the ideal city this threat is indeed quite serious.

The motifs that eventually emerge in Socrates' discussions of mimesis—perilous identification, weakening, depersonalization, castration, and so forth—play a key role in two important essays by Roger Caillois. In "La mante religieuse" ("The Praying Mantis") and "Mimétisme et Psychasthénie légendaire" ("Mimicry and Legendary Psychasthenia"), which appeared in the Surrealist journal *Minotaure* in 1934 and 1935, respectively, Caillois develops a conception of mimesis that harks back to as well as diverges from this Platonic tradition. We find precisely the same threatening scenarios that Socrates had feared. For Caillois mimesis is potentially debilitating, a case of flirtation that is seriously seductive. In particular, by means of a strong similarity that touches on identification, mimesis dissolves the border between the individual and its environment; hence the "psychasthenia" or the "weakening of the soul" that Caillois discerns as afflicting the very core of subjective identity. Along these lines Caillois displaces the phenomena of mimesis from the sphere of human consciousness and cognition to the nonverbal world of insect life. The circumvention of the human in favor of the nonhuman is of a piece with Caillois's general aesthetic program of the time. Throughout his association with André Breton and the Surrealists, Caillois sought a purely biological, noncognitive basis for artistic practice, especially for the surrealist practice of automatic writing.[5] In general he exhibited a strong interest in nonhuman forms of creativity, in an aesthetics emancipated from human forms of subjective, rational agency—perhaps an aesthetics of flirtation.

Regarding mimesis, both the psychasthenic effects and the creative but nonsubjective instincts could be discovered in the mimetic behavior of insects. Caillois's study on mimicry opens with the Socratic warning "Beware: Whoever pretends to be a ghost will turn into one [*Prends garde: à jouer au fantôme, on le devient*]!"[6] Implicit in the epigraph is the idea that the preservation of life depends on maintaining the differences, borders, and forms whereby the organism enjoys autonomy. As in Freud mimesis contributes to self-maintenance, but only when it is understood within a Platonic system grounded in dissimilar similarity. What Caillois observes among the insects is that mimesis or mimicry transgresses these very borders and therefore leads to self-loss. With this observation Caillois departs from the conventional biological research of his day to claim that insect mimicry has nothing to do with self-preservation or the preservation of the species. On the contrary, it often works against it. To support his claim he cites various scientific sources that show how mimetic behavior threatens the organism: "Numerous remains of mimetic insects are found in the stomach of predators. . . . Conversely, some inedible species, which therefore have nothing to fear, are mimetic. It seems we must therefore conclude with Cuénot that this is an 'epiphenomenon,' whose 'usefulness as a form of defense appears to be nil.'"[7] By drawing on the biological research of Lucien Cuénot, who, incidentally, referred to genes as "mnemons," Caillois concludes that natural camouflage does not serve any defensive purpose, nor does it present any attempt to distract. Among insects mimesis exhibits no functional use value.

For Caillois, because mimicry fulfills no purpose, because it fails to work as a means of self-preservation, it should be understood as a "luxury." Insofar as this luxurious uselessness may even lead to a complete loss of the physical self, it should also be regarded as "dangerous": "We are therefore dealing . . . with a dangerous luxury" (97). To demonstrate, he submits the case of the Phyllidae, whose bodies imitate leaves and thereby encourage other Phyllidae to ingest them: "This could almost be viewed as some sort of collective masochism culminating in mutual homophagy—with the imitation of the leaf serving as an incitement to cannibalism in this particular totem feast" (97). By imitating a leaf the insect becomes a leaf, an invitation for consumption. By blending in with its environment, the organism breaks out of the boundaries that define its individual distinctiveness.

Caillois famously attributes this process to the "luring appeal of space," where the environment itself becomes flirtatiously attractive. Lost in space—dissolved into space—the individual organism is no longer the origin of its movement; instead it constitutes only one point among others, a point, moreover, whose movement is determined by another source. In order to describe this process Caillois turns to the theories of the psychoanalyst Pierre Janet and the phenomenological psychiatrist Eugène Minkowski, who link the phenomenon of psychasthenia to a concept that expresses a will to be devoured by space, which for Caillois is nothing more than a "depersonalization through assimilation into space" (100): "This assimilation into space is inevitably accompanied by a diminished sense of personality and vitality. . . . Life withdraws to a lesser state. Sometimes, the identification is more than superficial: Phasmidae eggs resemble seeds not only in shape and color but also in terms of their internal biological structure" (101). Socrates' dismissive scenario, in which the image of Cratylus receives the divine gifts of motion, soul, and mind, here assumes concrete reality.

It is important to note that here mimesis does not denote artistic activity in the traditional sense of the word but rather an experiential process that is oddly passive. In this way Caillois combines the mimetic-metamorphic phenomenon observed among insects with psychical and physiological paralysis among humans.[8] Ultimately the mimetic drive should be regarded as an instinct of self-forgetfulness or self-loss—an instinct just as strong as, if not stronger than, the instinct of self-preservation. This does not mean, however, that for Caillois mimesis is an entirely negative concept. Precisely because mimicry blends the individual into its environment, it also serves as a basis for community. One can say that mimesis creates the common, insofar as the common is the nonprivate. As Quintilian defines it, "What is common with another ceases to be our own [*Quod commune cum alio est desinit esse proprium*]."[9] The *proper* (*proprium*) rightfully belongs to an individual; it is an individual's *property*; it cannot be taken away. It is therefore opposed to the *common*, which is indeed given away or surrendered. Forming a collective—joining a community—appears to entail some kind of sacrifice: a sacrifice of the purely *private*.

During his time in the Collège de Sociologie Caillois developed his theory of community in connection with the work of his colleague Georges Bataille.[10] According to Bataille, community is not based on the rationality of the useful but rather on the irrationality of the useless, that is, not on the instinct of self-preservation but on the instinct of self-loss. In his important article "The Notion of Expenditure," Bataille employs the theory of the gift that Marcel Mauss developed in relation to the phenomenon of the potlatch in order to distinguish two kinds of consumption: between productive consumption, which aims at the preservation of goods, property, and lives; and wasteful or luxurious consumption, which finds its purpose only in itself.[11] Luxury is grounded in the principle of loss. It is expenditure without compensation, without purpose. And the wasteful expenditure of goods, which certainly reached undreamed-of proportions among North American tribes, makes these goods sacred—a literal "sacrifice," the *sacri-ficium* that is performed by a loss of property, a loss of the *proprium*, of what is privately one's own. For this very reason sacrifice is the basis for community, just as, according to Bataille, the degradation of the Crucifixion led to the constitution of the Christian *ekklēsia*.[12]

For Caillois the "dangerous luxury" of mimesis is a sacrifice precisely in this sense, namely that it destroys the self as property. In his related study on the praying mantis, Caillois indicates how this sacrificial process is disclosed among the insects in the act of lovemaking. His memorable description seems itself to be motivated by a Cratylism, by a mimesis in language: The praying mantis (*la mante religieuse*) is the "religious lover" (*l'amante religieuse*) par excellence. As has been observed since Antiquity, in the act of copulation the female mantis, in one sudden movement, flicks off her lover's head and devours him. *L'amour* spells *la mort*: The male creature is lost in a momentary *Liebestod*. In his review of the scholarly literature,

Caillois is fascinated by the way scientists momentarily abandon "their professional dryness" and give in to the seduction of poetry. For example, he cites Léon Binet, a professor of physiology in Paris, who not only describes the insect as a "murderous mistress" but also supplements his observations by quoting the Romantic poet Alfred de Musset: "She exhausts, she kills, and this only makes her more beautiful [*Elle épuise, elle tue, et n'en est que plus belle*]."[13]

Above all what Caillois finds especially remarkable is that the male mantis, even after the decapitation and in a certain sense after its death, is capable of displaying what he calls the "objective" (that is, nonsubjective) "lyrical meaning of the praying mantis." In brief, even "when dead, [the mantis is] capable of simulating death" (79). In direct contrast to Freud, mimesis does not preclude a concrete confrontation with death; it does not allow a Platonic complacency grounded on the image's dissimilarity. The image of another's death cannot be written off as something "vapid and inane." On the contrary, the mimetic encounter discloses that the levity of amorous flirtation forecloses neither the gravest consequences nor the most ecstatic promises. In the blink of an eye, in the flick of a finger, flirtation can always lead to the luxurious danger of self-expenditure, not by losing its mimetic energy but precisely by maintaining it and intensifying it, without purpose and therefore without end.

WARTIME LOVE AFFAIRS AND DEATHLY FLIRTATION: FREUD AND CAILLOIS ON IDENTIFYING WITH LOSS

Sage Anderson

As a mode of social interaction, flirtation is commonly considered quite safe, at least compared to full-blown seduction. Skillfully managed, flirtation allows one to skirt commitment to any would-be relationship, deferring vulnerability as well as consummation to an unmet later date. However, flirtation also has the capacity to become something far more threatening; when a seemingly superficial back-and-forth with another is taken to the extremes of attraction, there emerges a profound danger of losing oneself altogether. In his essay "The Luxury of Self-Destruction," John Hamilton opens an inquiry into the opposition of flirtation and seduction with a reading of Freud's "Timely Thoughts on War and Death" (1915), zeroing in on an introductory passage from the second section, "Our Relationship to Death." It is here that Freud distinguishes between "an American flirtation, in which it is from the first determined that nothing is going to happen," and a "continental love affair in which both partners must constantly bear in mind the serious consequences."[1] In contrast to the empty gestures of flirtation, which mimic those of amorous seduction, the actual love affair—or seduction accomplished—makes of two autonomous parties a pair of mutually implicated partners.

From the outset, it is crucial to note that Freud's primary object of study in "Timely Thoughts" is not the soldiers actively engaged in combat but those people who stay at home and fear for the safety of their loved ones, a group "to which we ourselves belong."[2] The comparison of flirtation and seduction in this context serves to elucidate a change in the structure of psychological experience among the civilian population, wrought by the radically new kind of war that had recently broken out in Europe.[3] The metaphor is meant to demonstrate how living with war dramatically impacts one's relationship to death. Flirtation stands for incredulity, or making light of mortality, a peacetime posture that Freud associates with Americans. While it might be comfortable for us to assume that this is the richest perspective one could possibly have, the opposite is the case in Freud's view: A naïve attitude toward death effectively evacuates life of meaningful substance. As Hamilton puts it, by flirtatiously disbelieving in our own mortality, "we would rob ourselves of the opportunity to believe in self-preservation." This, then, is the opportunity provided by a continental love affair, which Freud uses as a figure for the physical and psychological confrontation with death that is brought home by World War I. Counterintuitively, vitality increases even as mortality takes stronger hold; newly faced with death, life is violently infused with consuming interest in itself. Hamilton paraphrases: "Prior to the great disenchantment triggered by the war and its unheard-of casualties, the ego did not truly believe in its own death and therefore did not believe in its own life."

I want to pursue this complex analogy between flirtation, seduction, life, and death back into the first section of Freud's "Timely Thoughts," "The Disappointment of War," where he deals with the perplexing persistence of war in cultivated, contemporary societies. According to Freud, World War I disappoints by disrupting the psychological illusion that humanity by now should have developed beyond war, or at least beyond any war that flagrantly defies conventional rules of combat (including consistently defined battlefields, mercy for the wounded, and exclusion of women and children from the fight).[4] Significantly for my discussion as it follows from Hamilton's reading, Freud's argument relies on self-limitation. In order to belong to the cultural community (*Kulturgemeinschaft*) of the great, world-dominant nation-states—and here, explicitly and reprehensibly, Freud defines such ruling bodies in terms of skin color[5]—one must limit the satisfaction of one's drives (*Triebbefriedigung*) through self-limitation (*Selbstbeschränkung*). In turn one enjoys state protection, enforced through the authoritative upholding of moral and ethical norms (*sittliche Normen*).[6] The illusion that we are actually content to live under such restraint conveniently covers the disturbingly aggressive desires that go unfulfilled in the altruistic individual as well as in the peaceable state.[7]

Extending the analogy, it is by limiting belligerent passions for the sake of self-protection that one behaves like the American flirt, evasively ensuring that nothing will ever happen. Thus protected, no one gets hurt. But no one goes home satisfied either. To make such frustrating compromise worthwhile, the individual wants to remain convinced that her normative self-limitation is reciprocated by the other party: "The cultural state [*Kulturstaat*] holds these ethical norms for the foundation of its continued existence. . . . So it would be assumed that it [the state] would want to respect them itself, and would not intend to undertake anything against them whereby it would contradict the grounding of its own subsistence."[8] What the state proscribes in the individual, the individual would like to imagine forgone by the state, especially when it comes to selfish deception and the wanton destruction of close neighbors. However, this comforting illusion is dealt a deathblow by the unprecedented experience of trench warfare. Freud challenges us to let go of our disappointment at the destruction of such illusions: "We must then accept without complaint that it [illusion] will one day hit against a piece of reality, on which it will smash [*zerschellen*]."[9] Inevitably, reality sets in at some point—for example, 1915 Vienna—and this should be no cause for complaint but rather an opportunity for self-examination. If the naïve illusion of having outgrown war falls on the side of flirtation, the disappointment of such illusion signals a shift into the maturity of seduction; the Great War as continental love affair drives home an expanded self-awareness, satisfying in its penetrating truthfulness. (It should be noted at this point that Freud admonishes against applying conclusions about the individual to mankind as a whole, which develops with drastic delays, albeit in parallel.)[10] Although the consequences of seduction are painful, the love affair is still worth it, as mere flirtation would perpetually preclude any substantial increase in self-realization. What stands to be gained from the disappointment of war is a more honest relationship to death. For Freud, when the illusion of peaceable satiation goes to smash, this breach allows the ego to more accurately comprehend life at its limits. At these limits, not only must the individual die, she also wants to kill.

A pressing question arises in this context: What does it means to flirt with death? Colloquially we say that someone flirts with death by courting needless danger or taking stupid risks—tempting fate, so to speak. This is consistent with "Timely Thoughts" to the extent that flirtation in Freud's model entails a foreclosure of consequence, an unpronounced determination that each individual will emerge intact, ego unscathed, from any shallow encounter with another, be it playing at romance in a social setting or psychologically parrying with the thought of death. This is the value of self-limitation; thrillingly much can be ventured when there is no fear of loss. After all, if nothing is going to happen in the end—if indeed there is no end in sight or purpose in mind—then anything goes for now. However, flirtation with death may be taken much further if one is willing to risk more of oneself. For Hamilton, crucially, the opposition of flirtation and seduction hinges on the relationship between self-limitation and mimesis. The "mimetic image" makes all the difference or none at all. Freud's metaphor shows more than his own argument acknowledges about the flirtation with death; this plays out in the defense mechanism provided by the "dissimilar similarity" that allows one thing to be *like* another while remaining distinct unto itself.

Prior to World War I it was possible—*only* possible, according to Freud—to relate to death through mimetic representation, with the security provided by aesthetic distance from the scene of fatality. In the passage following the one that Hamilton cites, Freud refers to this irretrievable past perspective as though it were still present: "Thus it cannot happen otherwise but that we seek compensation for the forfeits of life in the world of fiction, in literature, in theater. There we still find people who understand how to die, indeed, who even manage to kill one another."[11] Seeking out fictional representations, one is able to vicariously participate in death without dying or killing, identifying without internalizing what it is to die or kill. The reader or theatergoer is like the flirt in this respect. Hamilton writes, "Just as the flirt imitates the serious lover, so the serious implications of one's own annihilation can be flirted away by means of imitation." The similarity between reading about or watching a character die in a novel or play and flirting with a stranger at a party lies in one's psychological remove from the underlying motivation of each situation (annihilation and sex, respectively). Picturing oneself as the hero or heroine of a murderous plot or *pretending* to lose oneself in the heat of the moment—in German *so tun, als ob* (to act as if)—one comes pleasurably close to tantalizing risk while holding any real threat to bodily integrity at arm's length. This strategy of living out desire through representation would seem as sustainable as it is appealing, both interpersonally and aesthetically. Yet in the context of his 1915 essay,[12] Freud insists that life gains in vital significance what is stripped away of disinterested illusion. The psyche must expand to accommodate harsher truths, and this is what happens when the proliferation of war makes death so present that it defies all representation.

In the course of his discussion Hamilton pulls back from Freud in order to push the significance of flirtation a step further; rather than setting representation against reality, he foregrounds his reading of Roger Caillois by problematizing the very notion of mimesis that allows this distinction to stay fixed. In so doing, Hamilton reiterates a deep-seated cultural fear voiced since Plato,[13] namely the fear that imitation may negate the difference constitutive of identity. *Acting as if* may already be going too far, in which case flirtation no longer appears so safe. Indeed, cast in this light, imitation constitutes a grave threat to the individual as well as the republic. Fundamental power structures are in jeopardy; underlying the fear of imitation is a characteristically masculine panic at the prospect of a traditionally feminized weakness.[14] Hamilton writes, "Face-to-face with mimesis, both the sovereignty of the subject and the subjectivity of the sovereign appear to be at risk, exposed to utter dismantling." Mimesis thus results in a blurring of precisely those boundaries that it is employed to reinforce, namely the boundaries that define sovereign and subject as distinct entities.

Once the divisions of the human individual have been effectively blurred, Hamilton introduces what he calls "an aesthetics of flirtation" in the work of Caillois.[15] Uncertain of ourselves as sovereign subjects, we are further made to see that we are living among insects, and have been all along. The focus is on two dense essays, "La mante réligieuse" ("The Praying Mantis") and "Mimétisme et Psychasthénie légendaire" ("Mimicry and Legendary Psychasthenia"). These essays were first published separately in the central Surrealist organ *Minotaure*, in 1934 and 1935, respectively. Together they were republished in 1938 in the book *Le mythe et l'homme*, shortly after the foundation of the Collège de Sociologie by Caillois, Georges Bataille, and others.[16] I will restrict my attention to "Mimicry and Legendary Psychasthenia" in order to explore the implications of flirtation as a mimetic form, leaving aside the image immediately called to mind by "The Praying Mantis"—that of the decapitated postcoital male mantis—as an obscene reminder of seduction's gravest consequences.

Caillois begins his argument in "Mimicry and Legendary Psychasthenia" with a detailed classification of mimetic defense mechanisms in the animal kingdom, ranging from the white fur of mammals living in the snow to the gray-green spots and transparent streaks on the wings of butterflies that alight on leaves marred by moss and mold. All of this can be scientifically explained in terms of natural selection, but according to Caillois, existing explanations depend on an anthropomorphic perspective that largely fails to account for phenomena of resemblance in their extreme complexity and excessive precision. As Caillois claims and Hamilton emphasizes, resemblance in the magnified habitat of insects does not always or only serve the defensive purpose of self-preservation. The most telling example is that of the Phyllies (family *Phylliidae*, commonly known as leaf insects); these insects resemble their habitat so closely that they have been known to graze on each other inadvertently, herbivores turned cannibals in an undifferentiated riot of leafy green. "By imitating a leaf the insect becomes a leaf," is Hamilton's concise phrasing. Such insects demonstrate how imitation may serve to effectively negate the difference that defines an individual organism; what comes to the fore is the fascination of an organism's most extreme assimilation to its milieu, in the material sense of background.[17] Hamilton highlights Caillois's characterization of imitation as a "dangerous luxury": "Among insects mimesis exhibits no functional use value." Thus defying common generalization of economic principles along evolutionary lines, mimicry is sometimes the opposite of self-promoting.

Caillois pursues this line of thinking in a series of heavily documented examples to arrive at the notion of "legendary psychasthenia," a phrase he coins to explain processes of "depersonalization by assimilation to space."[18] Etymologically, psychasthenia connotes a weakening of *psyche*, as in breath, spirit, or soul. *Entomologically*, it designates such nonuseful mimesis as would make the insect one with the leaf that it eats. Caillois closes his essay by pointing to parallels in human psychology, with reference to pathological cases and lyric literature, "where psychoanalysis sees the expression of a kind of regret for prenatal unconsciousness."[19] Teasing out the aesthetic and political implications of psychasthenia, Hamilton brings into focus "an experiential process that is oddly passive." The minute mimetic precision that lets animal life recede quiescently into vegetation may shed light on human patterns of thought and behavior that tend toward "self-forgetfulness or self-loss—an instinct just as strong as, if not stronger than, the instinct of self-preservation." In other words, reimplicating Freud at a later stage, mimesis ultimately leads beyond the pleasure principle.[20]

But how do passivity and self-loss fit into the model of flirtation as opposed to seduction? In the scenarios at hand, similarity no longer brings one thing close to another thing *like* it but rather allows the first thing to bleed into that other thing, relinquishing self-preserving difference by overstepping proximity into exactitude. This would seem to reverse the opposition as parsed thus far, landing us along with mimetic insects squarely in the territory of seduction rather than flirtation. Indeed, Caillois invokes seduction in his description of psychasthenic phenomena: "In these conditions, one conceives that unorganized space does not cease to exercise *a sort of seduction* on it [the insect or organism], continuing to weigh it down, to hold onto it, always ready to take it back in order to make up for the difference at the level that isolates the organic in the inorganic."[21] What humans take to be the distinguishing marks of an individual or species turn out to be marks of indistinction as the insect is received into unorganized space. This is most perfectly exemplified by certain types of grasshoppers whose forewings cover the rear of the body to look like a leaf that has been partially eaten by a grasshopper.[22] For Caillois, the plethora of such extreme, excessive examples demonstrates "a sort of seduction" that underlies "the material indistinction of the being and its milieu."[23] Hamilton argues, however, this is no seduction but rather a convincing demonstration of the unrealized potential of flirtation. The danger of mimesis is at once its draw; letting go of the death grip on self-identity, individuals may be able to come together to form an aesthetic community. With reference to Bataille's "Notion of Expenditure," Hamilton finally points to the basis for community in "the *sacri-ficium* that is performed by a loss of property, a loss of . . . what is privately one's own." Flirtation, as mimesis intensified, proves to be the kind of dangerous luxury that creates shared space, thus opening up aesthetic possibilities that go beyond the protection of dissimilar similarity into radically common territory.

In sum, the opposition between flirtation and seduction stands or falls with the status of mimesis. If imitation is a means of maintaining difference, then there is no danger in flirting; the object of representation, be it romantic partnership or death, will always remain at bay. If, on the other hand, mimicry equates to identification, then nothing even resembling seduction is safe. Yet the latter outcome may prove the more desirable, if also the more dangerous. With the disappointment of the illusion of self-preservation comes the opportunity to lose oneself to greater effect. When distinction yields to similarity, getting close is already getting together. By embracing the thought that there is no difference, one may find a more direct way to approach others, and in flirting with death, a less isolated way to live.

The . . . perspective of a countless multitude of worlds as it were annihilates my importance as an *animal creature.*
— Immanuel Kant, *Critique of Practical Reason*

On the contrary, the lizard has *its own relation* to the rock, to the sun, and to a host of other things.
— Martin Heidegger, *The Fundamental Concepts of Metaphysics*

BESTIALITY: MEDIATION *MORE FERARUM*

Jacques Lezra

A young archaeologist develops an attachment to an ancient bas-relief, unidentified, that he has seen in a museum in Rome. He buys a simulacrum; he calls the figure Gradiva, the beautiful walker; she hangs on his wall. A terrible, anxious dream places the lovely Gradiva in Pompeii, at the moment of the eruption of Vesuvius. Our protagonist travels to the excavation some time later and finds there, in the Casa di Meleagro, a young woman who bears, he believes, a startling resemblance to the figure from Rome, from his wall, from his dream. He pursues her through the dig and convinces himself that she is a creature of flesh and blood rather than a statue or a ghost. They talk, they flirt, *oeillades* are exchanged, and she reveals that she knows his name, Norbert Hanold. Zoe Bertgang—this is Gradiva *rediviva*'s name—turns out to be a childhood friend and former neighbor, the daughter of an eccentric zoologist who is now interested primarily in pursuing the research of a colleague, someone called Eimer, on a species of lizard found on the island of Capri. Zoe had a strong crush on Norbert as an adolescent; over the course of the time they spend together among the ruins of Pompeii, Norbert discovers behind his

125

own infatuation with the figure of Gradiva his old attraction to Zoe. An archaeology of his affective life has revealed, behind the plaster cast of an archaic, nameless spirit, the living object of his earliest affections. The novel ends happily: Flirtation leads to a torrid encounter among the ruins (prudishly hinted at rather than described), passion passes on to engagement, and Freud's analysis begins in earnest.[1]

Let's line up the story, and Freud's reading and uses of it, with our subject matter. On one hand, the path leading from a first glance, a flirtatious look, to its outcome stretches before and behind us ontogenetically and phylogenetically. A glance leads to or flows from the true, or primary, object we desire; we take steps from that first *oeillade* to consummation on an old, stony path. What we see is conditioned by what we remember ancestrally: the mother's love, fear and envy of the father, and so on. Even more rigorously: We glance at, flirt with that and only that which will yield, out of the apparent immediacy and apparent circumstantiality of our passing glance, the old and primary object. Flirtation, by this description, leaves us untouched and leaves the other at whom we gaze untouched as well. Whatever passes between us is set already before us: When we flirt we are discovering again what was already immediate in us and acting out an old script: Flirtation is, by this description, the form of desire's immanence.

This is the story we would be inclined to read—and we do throughout Freud, across the various topologies, explicitly and implicitly. Freud draws some consequences for us, and others he leaves more or less implicit, as for instance the glaring thought that the discipline of psychoanalysis itself, to the extent that it depends on the mechanics of the transference, is a sort of arrested *oeillade*, a complex double flirtation, where glances are exchanged between the unconscious of one and another figure in the analytic scenario, carefully guarded from consummation by the breathless, petrifying armature of the therapeutic frame, ethical norms, lexicon, and expectation.

At that strange crossroads that is Freud's analysis of Wilhelm Jensen's novella *Gradiva* there stands also another figure, the mediating figure of the animal that desires and is desired, whose custom, habit, or culture it is to express its desire as beasts do, *more bestiarum* or, as Freud more often says, *more ferarum,* an expression he uses most famously in the "Wolf Man," where the scene of the parents' midafternoon coition "a tergo, more ferarum" is reconstructed by the analyst and the patient from the patient's wolf dream and ancillary matters.[2] Bestiality or ferality, yes, of course, lurid and eternally provocative, the scandalous crossing of the line between species; a final insult to the taxonomic norm; a complicated wound to species narcissism. At the same time and perhaps less evidently, a lurid and provocative topic precisely inasmuch as all human coupling, all human-human relations occur *more ferarum,* at least in the sense that human animals are also beasts, *ferae.* We flirt, and whether we know it or not, whether we choose it or not, when we do so we are imagining the parents' energetic movement, fitting ourselves into the primal scene's syntax and topology, into its taxonomy. We assume the quadrupedal stance of the mother, the analytical and practical requirement that the father's penetration be *a tergo* so that both sets of genital organs lie exposed to our regard and to the little witness's astonished gaze. On this path flirtation is not only and always structurally heterosexual; it is also and always structurally *bestial.* The affective archaeology of human life necessarily passes through the figure of the nonhuman animal and through the primal figure of parental coupling.

Yes, this is the story we'd be inclined to read throughout Freud.[3] But it is not the only story, and it isn't the one I'm going to focus on, briefly, here. *Passes through*: We presume that the old Oedipal path and the equally old path of the beasts can be mapped onto one another without loss; we assume that human and animal taxonomies do indeed mimic one another; we understand indeed that the human is a species of the larger genus, the *animal.* It is on these conditions that our glances cross, that we follow the immanent path that desire has always already set before us. *Passes through*: But do these conditions in fact obtain? Or does one figure or one path, the path

of the human animal and the path on which animals couple *more ferarum*, cross out, interrupt, block the other? Each passing through, clearing but also blocking the other: A first glance enacts desire's immanent form immediately but also leads us away, across competing taxonomies, where we want unthinkable monsters and chimeras and find ourselves as a result as wild and unclassifiable as they. Mediation *more ferarum*.

Let's switch registers and say that there are two roads through Freud's reading of the Gradiva story. The first lies between the proper object of affection or disaffection and the improper, fetishistic, arresting, or traumatizing one. Here the vectors we describe are not chronological but positional. Gradiva's image, unnamed at the story's opening, recast and reproduced, captures the archaeologist's attention; his affections will now be directed toward love objects that resemble that image or bring it to mind, though they will all be found to be lacking inasmuch as they are not that image: They are alive. The memory of Norbert's face, of her adolescent infatuation with him, and of the loss of that object when Norbert's attention turns from Zoe to the study of archaeology—all these in turn fix Zoe's attention on her father, the man whose place Norbert should have taken but did not, but whose eccentric attributes Norbert shares; indeed it is these very attributes, resulting in a fixation on archaeology in Norbert's case and on zoology in her father's, that have driven Norbert from her.

The second path that Freud traces for us is the path on which human animals take the place of nonhuman animals: canaries, flies, and especially lizards.[4] Here are two moments. The first, Zoe's father's exclamation to Norbert:

> He turned his head, as Norbert came close to him, looked at the latter in surprise for a moment and then said, "Are you interested in *Faraglionensis*? I should hardly have supposed it, but it seems thoroughly probable that they are found not only in the *Faraglioni* of Capri, but also dwell permanently on the mainland."[5]

And this is Zoe reflecting on her father's dotty lizard love:

> From my early years, I have been sure that a woman is of use in the world only when she relieves a man of the trouble of deciding household matters; I generally do this for my father and therefore you can also be rather at ease about your future. Should he, however, by chance, in this case, have an opinion different from mine, we will make it as simple as possible. You go over to Capri for a couple of days; there, with a grass snare—you can practice making them on my little finger— catch a *lacerta Faraglionensis*. Let it go here again, and catch it before his eyes. Then give him free choice between it and me, and you will have me so surely that I am sorry for you.[6]

Jensen establishes a taxonomy of his own by revealing the kinship between Norbert the archaeologist, Zoe's zoologist father, and the narrator, who slyly categorizes them together as well: All three are members of a peculiar superspecies, the superspecies of animals bent on classification. Their rage for order has communicated itself to Gradiva *rediviva*, to Zoe, a taxonomic impulse that has passed itself on like an acquired characteristic inherited by the child, or like another's secret that she bears encrypted within her. For Zoe also employs this taxonomic imagination not only to refer to her father's preferred lizard but also, like the narrator, to classify Norbert and her father in the same *taxon*.

But there is more here. Freud makes much of Jensen's identification of Zoe, the figure of life, with the curious, lithe *Lacerta Faraglionensis*, the lizard that she teaches Norbert how to catch, having learned that lesson from her father, who learned it from his "colleague" Eimer. Zoe teaches Norbert to catch the lizard so that he will be able to catch her as well, to take her from the domestic ecology of the exclusive father-daughter relation. In order to have her father deliver her to Norbert, she teaches Norbert to deliver to her father nature's, and Jensen's, figure for her: the lizard. She delivers herself in person to Norbert by delivering herself, in lizard shape, through Norbert to her father. This is not, though, just any old lizard. The blue lizard of Capri, *Lacerta Faraglionensis*, known also as *Podarcis sicula coerulea*, was first described comprehensively in 1872 by a controversial zoologist by the name, of course, of Theodor Eimer, who (as he put it in the 1898 *On Orthogenesis: And the Impotence of Natural Selection in Species Formation*) "found [in *Lacerta Faraglionensis*] an animal which might be with equal justice described as species or variety [*als Art wie als Abart bezeichnen*], so much does it differ from the original form."[7]

Lacerta Faraglionensis, it turns out, is not just beautiful; it is also a taxonomic puzzle that occupies a very special place in the late nineteenth-century debates between Darwinian and Lamarckian evolutionary biologists. Gradiva/Zoe's identification with this taxonomic "aberration," as Eimer calls the lizard, which is neither a variety nor a species but somehow both, is crucial—and because of it we now understand Zoe's strange role in Jensen's story as both the subject of classification and its object, both the animal classifying the field of knowledge and an animal classified within the field of knowledge. We cannot settle whether her drive to classify and identify, to classify or identify herself among other animals and to identify and classify the men in her life, is a species attribute or a variety attribute. Nor can it be settled whether she derives this quality of taxonomic overdetermination from her father's *mores* or from her heredity. Zoe, the figure of life, retains control over her identity, asserts it—identifying herself with the lizard, assuming the lizard's taxonomic curiosity, its uniqueness both within the zoological world and within the taxonomic reconstruction of that world, its disciplinary map. Zoe/Gradiva is a *hapax* species. For Jensen, though, when Zoe associates herself with the strange lizard that her father seeks, telling Norbert to visit the Faraglioni rock, catch a blue lizard, release it on land, and then catch it in order to offer her father the choice between herself and the lizard, when she does all this she threatens to wreak havoc on Eimer's thesis—that the characteristics the lizard acquires develop on the island and are passed on as acquired characteristics, orthogenetically, by transplanting the lizard to the mainland, where it would have had an entirely different habitat and its characteristic color and psychological docility would have been inexplicable in evolutionary terms. But *she*, Zoe, is there already, herself: The havoc she has wrought on the evolutionary taxonomy that Freud describes shifts into the philosophical domain. When Gradiva/Zoe hands herself off to Norbert as a lizard, when she allows herself to be weighed in the same scales as the blue lizard of Capri, she turns her father's decision (to give his daughter away or not) and her lover's decision (to accept the daughter, to seek her father's permission or not) into nondecisions by giving herself to both of her lovers, both men, by means of the same gesture. Making her father's seeming choice the mere choice between her human figure and her beastly one, giving herself to Norbert as a lizard so that he will have her as a woman, she is, in short, able to reduce their choices to the spurious choice between functionally identical terms. When Zoe/Gradiva teaches her lover how to force her father to deliver her to Norbert, she is effectively destroying the capacity to *decide* or to choose that we associate with the nomological, with the Kantian strain of classical deontological ethics. Choices of this sort—for instance, the choice to become domesticated or acculturated, to take on a name and step into a taxonomy—these choices are not themselves part of the *nomos*. But are they part of an ecological *ethos*?

When he closes his analysis of the novella, Freud draws his reader's attention to the following lovely passage from *Gradiva*. It is here that he answers the question of whether the animal at the crossroads, the *bestial* animal at the crossroads, is on the same path as the old man we encounter on the road from Delphos to Thebes, whether the two paths cross on the side of *ethos* or of *nomos*. Here too Freud gives us the means of addressing the place of psychoanalysis in, among, before, beyond the other human sciences. Zoe is speaking to Norbert:

> When archaeology overcame you . . . I imagined that you had become an intolerable person, who had no longer, at least for me, an eye in his head, a tongue in his mouth, nor any of the memories that I retained of our childhood friendship. . . . To you I was but air, and you, with your shock of light hair, which I had formerly pulled so often, were as boresome, dry and tongue-tied as a stuffed cockatoo and at the same time as grandiose as an—archaeopteryx; I believe the excavated, antediluvian bird-monster is so called; but that your head harbored an imagination so magnificent as here in Pompeii to consider me something excavated and restored to life—I had not surmised that of you, and when you suddenly stood before me unexpectedly, it cost me some effort at first to understand what kind of incredible fancy your imagination had invented. Then I was amused.[8]

About these lines Freud says:

> When Zoë pictures for us the transformation of the playmate of her youth, which seems so sad for her, she insults him by a comparison with the archaeopteryx, that bird-monster which belongs to the archaeology of zoölogy. So she has found a single, concrete expression for identifying the two people; her resentment strikes the beloved as well as the father with the same word. The archaeopteryx is, so to speak, the compromise, or intermediary representation in which the folly of her beloved coincides with her thought of an analogous folly of her father.[9]

This "single, concrete expression for identifying the two people" is the archaeopteryx—a composite, archaic version of the other, unique figure that Zoe/Gradiva is also, the lizard. But the archaeopteryx is more again. A "single, concrete expression," the archaic bird serves to identify or condense not just "people" from Zoe/Gradiva's psychic menagerie but also levels of Freud's argument. The archaeopteryx is the lizard, transformed; it is where Zoe/Gradiva's father and her lover meet; it is the figure that an emerging psychoanalytic establishment uses to designate empirical science, bringing together zoology and archaeology but also relegating them jointly, as one beast, to the pre-history of scientific inquiry, to a prehistory paradoxically concerned only with the surface of human behavior and of animal behavior. And the archaeopteryx is Freud's figure, or Jensen's figure, for a form of "expression" or a figure of thought that, however useful it is for representing these sorts of "compromise-representations," must itself be set aside or overcome. In place of the "*Kompromiß- oder Mittelvorstellung*" represented by the petrified bird and its living counterpart, the extraordinary lizard of the Mediterranean islands, psychoanalysis provides a different "expression," no longer "concrete," no longer a compromise or a mean or median representation between two established ordering systems or taxonomies, archaeology and zoology. For Zoe/Gradiva's identification of "two people" is not, or not only, a species or a variety of pathology, to be diagnosed and classified by the wily narrator or by Freud, the even wilier reader. Such "identifications" of course occur: They are the flickering substance of our every desire, which is always archaeologically shaped and haunted by residual objects, fossils that crop up in part among and within our love objects only to become disengaged, fly off, dehisce.

When an identification of one figure with another suffers arrest, when the long-dead figure I desire becomes as it were set in stone, or when my libidinal expression becomes fixed on an improper or unconventional spot or identity—in this situation pathological forms of repetition are installed, symptomatologies built, a pathology identified, classified, rendered treatable. Taxonomy, in short, is on this level the effect and the symptom of an arrested substitution, of a too concrete form of *Kompromiß- oder Mittelvorstellung*. But the bestial figure of and for *mediation* that Freud finds among the ruins is not amenable to "concrete" expression. It is neither *Art* nor *Abart*; the name Eimer is neither fictional nor historical alone, nor only a proper name *or* the name of a household device, but it is not, or not simply, both at once (as the archaeopteryx is at the same time part of zoology and part of archaeology), since its being in one place, fiction, destroys the truth claims in the other. Yes, the possibility that the blue lizard of Capri should be found on the mainland, or brought forcibly to the mainland only to be "discovered" there scientifically, destroys the principles of taxonomy and the evolutionary principles the lizard helped to establish. But this is trivial; other taxonomies are found; *Art* and *Abart* are kept distinct on the production of further, intervening species or variants. Freud's mediation, or flirtation with and as the beasts do it, *more ferarum*, holds modes of description, causation, determination, and history in tense, dynamic, and blocked exchange.[10] It is not only that *any* discovery, regardless of the discipline, whether zoology, archaeology, or psychoanalysis, is from this point on open to the most severe skeptical inquiry. No, what seems to me scandalous, even appalling, about Freud's *more ferarum* is not primarily the epistemological quandaries into which it leads us. I mention that Zoe enjoins or invites her lover to take her substitute, her image, the lizard, from one frame or ecology to another—and I noted earlier that this injunction, or invitation, amounts to a spurious, merely *seeming* trade destined to keep Zoe/Gradiva's desires intact and distributed across the complex surface of the masculine Oedipal drama in which lover, father, intended, and even the remote zoologist Eimer are involved.

Mediation *more ferarum* forces us to frame the answers to disciplinary and epistemological questions outside the domain of classical normative ethics, outside the heteronormative primal scenes in which it has classically developed, and within the horizon of questions that Freud notoriously, constantly, pervasively *could not think*,

whose answers lie like moving footsteps across the body of his works: what the nonhuman animal wants; what it means to decouple sexual object choice from the old, stony path of Oedipus. If we are to operate on *this* register—in the domain of the reproduction of Zoe/Gradiva's desires—we will need to amend, severely, Kant's lovely lines from the close of the *Critique of Practical Reason*. For after Freud we will find that the perspective, the *oeillade* of the *animal creature* enjoins us, or invites us, to smuggle what we call "decision," "autonomy," and "responsibility" from the off-coast preserve of normative ethics back onto the disciplinary mainland from which it has been separated since Kant. After Freud we are invited, or enjoined, to acknowledge that we are driven to acts and decisions not by principle alone or mainly, nor by the love of wisdom, not in the main by philosophical or scientific desire, but also and determiningly according to the custom of the beasts, according to the customary ethos of the animal, because some animal winks fetchingly at us.

DOING IT AS THE BEASTS DID:
INTERTEXTUALITY AS FLIRTATION IN *GRADIVA*

Barbara Natalie Nagel

Flirtation is a concept defined by its latency. This means, on the one hand, that flirtation ceases to be flirtation when it transgresses a taboo and gives itself to consummation. Instead flirtation hovers over—but doesn't cross—the line of distinction between hypothetical and realized desire. On the other hand, flirtation isn't simply the opposite of transgression because it structurally depends on the forbidden to give momentum to the flirt. Adam Phillips, who wrote *On Flirtation*, elaborates on this ambivalence that is inherent in the concept of flirtation: "Flirtation confirms the connection between excitement and uncertainty."[1] The flirt always flirts with the serious without, however, taking itself too seriously.

The author of "Bestiality: Mediation *More Ferarum*," Jacques Lezra, is generally known from his writings as someone who goes right for the extreme.[2] One may therefore be curious as to what he comes up with when dealing with a more restrained topic, such as flirtation. The answer is: He goes for the extreme—with a paper on bestiality, fetishism, incest, necrophilia, sadomasochism, and patricide in Wilhelm Jensen's *Gradiva*. Lezra is not the first to push the obscene implications of Jensen's novella; there is, for example, Alain Robbe-Grillet's sultry drama *Gradiva (C'est Gradiva qui vous appelle)* from 2006, which literalizes the sadomasochistic implications of Jensen's novella and at the same time inverts the gender dynamics by presenting bloody tableaux of compliant young women. Obviously this comparison does not do justice to Lezra's rigor, his imaginativeness, and, yes, his ability to surprise us. In light of what Lezra and Robbe-Grillet bring out, however, and in light of what I have just said on the relation between flirtation and transgression, one wonders whether *Gradiva* can still be called a flirtatious text. I would argue that it can be. Maybe we could nuance Lezra's argument (shared implicitly by Robbe-Grillet) by showing the novella's unacknowledged tension between flirtation and obscenity, that is, its latent obscenity. The question is how Jensen manages to maintain a tension between flirtation and obscenity. What is the economy between the invisible and the visible, between ambiguous and literalized desire, the implicit and explicit? Or, shorter: What keeps the flirtation from turning into excess?

On a linguistic level it is the subjunctive, that is, the fictionalizing mode of *as if*, that saves Jensen's fantastic piece (his *Phantasiestück*) from censorship. This *as if* produces a sense of "hesitation" in the reader, acknowledged by Derrida in his brief, spectral reading of *Gradiva*.[3] One could also say that the mode of *as if* allows for a certain skepticism that is crucial for flirtation to function, for "the virtues . . . of being uncommitted," as Phillips has it.[4] In any case it is remarkable that Jensen's story makes use of the formulation *as if* (*als ob*) no less than twenty times. On the level of plot a young man called Norbert falls in love with an ancient relief of a young woman because of the way she walks. Yet he behaves only *as if* he were a pervert. The protagonist turns out to be too repressed to admit to himself that his obsession with the archaeological piece is just a cover-up for his continuing love for his childhood friend Zoe. *Gradiva*, we conclude, in this linguistic regard only flirts with the obscene.

But then what about the animals, and the various registers of bestiality that Lezra masterfully unfolds before our eyes? How can a text crowded with winking animals still be flirtatious? The fact that Lezra focuses on, of all things, the bestial, animal moments in *Gradiva* to show how flirtation functions is likely to be perceived as at least counterintuitive. This goes with a tendency in animal studies to read animals either as allegorical or pedagogical figures in fables, or, inspired by the Deleuzian notion of "becoming-animal," to take the animal as a last resort of "the real." Lezra resists the latter, literalizing and romanticizing tendency just as he avoids the pitfalls of the former, narrowly allegorical approach toward animal representations. According to Lezra's reading of Freud's reading of Jensen, desire always goes through "the mediating figure of the animal that desires and is desired, whose custom, habit, or culture it is to express its desire as beasts do, *more bestiarum*." The object of flirtation thus doesn't matter because we are only acting out a script, and a bestial one at that.

And yet if desire is itself only when it desires the animal (in us), then we face a paradox, for it is only on account of the *medial* function of the animal that our desire can become *immediate*. Likewise flirtation in Lezra's reading of *Gradiva* is characterized by "the apparent immediacy and apparent circumstantiality of our passing glance." I am interested in this "circumstantiality" and how it relates to the animal figures in *Gradiva* because to me flirtation is not so much about the drive as about the tempering and the restraint of the drive. I would like to take up Lezra's hypothesis that animals function as instances of mediation and try to push this claim a little further by introducing examples in which animals in *Gradiva* work as instances not only of mediation but of *double* mediation. Lezra showed that in Jensen's novella our desire goes through the animal; I intend to show that the animal's desire too goes through the animal. More concretely Jensen's animals invoke animals from other literary texts; they function as moments of intertextuality. To say this is to understand intertextuality as yet another dimension of mediation and as yet another form of flirtation. Intertextuality as a procedure is based on repetition, just as flirtation as a mimetic *techne* is also inherently repetitive. There are moments when we find ourselves wondering whether a certain text is repeating another text's gestures, and there are moments when we wonder whether someone else is engaging in a flirtatious play with us by picking up on our own words and gestures. What keeps the flirtation alive in both cases—the textual as well as the creaturely one—is that we can't tell if the repetition we perceive is "real" or if we are just imagining a correspondence between two (or more) bodies, two (or more) texts. In this specific constellation, flirtation indeed can take the shape of a repeated winking between people, animals, texts.

In order to sustain my claim let me introduce a bestial scene of flirtation from *Gradiva*, a scene that Lezra does not mention. It is Zoe (the real girl whom Norbert mistakes for the Gradiva) who flirts with Norbert by pretending to be the legendary Pompeian girl. Toward the end of the story Norbert surprises Zoe by joining the flirt. The script of the scene affirms Lezra's thesis that lizards, canaries, flies, all of these are the occasion for flirtation through Jensen's story. But at the end of *Gradiva* a fly becomes not only a medium but a double medium of flirtation. "There the fly sits again!" Norbert calls, "The fly—where?" Zoe asks.

> "There on your cheek!" and immediately the man, as he answered, wraps his arm around her neck all of a sudden and snapped at the insect, this time with his lips. . . . Apparently, however, without success for right afterwards he cried again, "No, now it's on your lips" and thereupon, quick as a flash, he directed thither his attempt to capture, now remaining so long that no doubt could survive that he succeeded in completely accomplishing his purpose."[5]

The fly, however, may not be the only animal in the scene: There might be a lizard in the picture too. After all, Norbert did not simply kiss Zoe but actually snapped (*haschte*) a fly off her lips, like a lizard eating a fly.[6] We do not know for certain whether Norbert is becoming a lizard and indulging in an act of bestiality or is only flirting, that is, only *pretending* to be a lizard when he wraps himself around Zoe (*sich um sie schlang*, a verb that adds another animal to the scene:

a snake, *Schlange*). Speaking of pretending, a practice densely inter-
twined with that of flirtation, it seems no coincidence that Austin in
his essay "On Pretending" offers the example of someone pretending to be an animal: During a game a man acts as if he were a hyena
but then bites off "a fair-sized piece right out of" the narrator's calf.
Austin warns, "This sort of thing in these circumstances will not pass
as '(only) pretending to be a hyena.' True—but then neither will it
pass as *really being* a hyena."[7] Just like Lezra, Austin too is neither
satisfied with interpreting the scene as a mere representation of an
animal, nor does he want to read it as an instant of becoming-animal.
Instead Austin problematizes how certain behaviors may challenge
the very limits of how we define *pretending*. But why does he pick
an animal to illustrate this situation? For Lezra "all human-human
relations occur *more ferarum*, at least in the sense that human animals are also beasts, *ferae*. We flirt, and whether we know it or not,
whether we choose it or not, when we do so we are imagining the
parents' energetic movement, fitting ourselves into the primal scene's
syntax and topology, into its taxonomy." If flirtation thus always goes
through the animal, then we never pretend to be anything *but* an
animal when we flirt. More generally when it comes to aggression
qua sexual aggression, as in Austin's example, it seems indeed as if
the animal is *the* medium for the desire for the immediate.

And yet the fly-snapping kiss scene in *Gradiva* is anything but immediate in its communication. Instead it seems to take a detour via
an older text from the German canon, *the* German text on romantic, unrequited love. When Norbert, the lizard, snaps a fly from Zoe's
lips, the lizard functions as a double medium insofar as the lizard
could be read as a medium for another animal that is a medium. I am
thinking of Goethe's *The Sorrows of Young Werther* because Zoe, just
like Lotte, owns a yellow canary, a fact to which Jensen's story re-
turns repeatedly. Recall the scene when Lotte introduces to Werther
her little yellow friend:

> "He kisses me too, look!" As she held the small creature to her mouth, it
> pressed itself so captivatingly on those sweet lips, as if it could have felt

the happiness it was enjoying. "He shall kiss you too," she said and handed the bird over to me. The little beak made its way from her lips to mine, and the pecking touch was like a breath, an intimation, of loving enjoyment. Its kiss, I said, is not entirely without desire, it is seeking food and withdrawing dissatisfied from the empty caress. "He eats from my mouth," too, she said.—She offered it a few crumbs with her lips, from which the joys of innocently devoted love smiled in complete bliss. I turned my face away. She should not do this![8]

In his essay "Flirtation," Georg Simmel writes that flirtation "is fond of utilizing what might be called extraneous objects: dogs, flowers, children." Here it is a canary that seems to have the function of demonstrating to Werther "how enviable the apparent object is."[9] The canary "kisses" Lotte by picking a breadcrumb from her lips. If we now return to *Gradiva*, the breadcrumb[10] on Lotte's lips could be substituted with the fly in Jensen's story; the position of the hungry canary would then be occupied by a lizard-like Norbert. This claim could be sustained by several moments toward the beginning of the story, where already Norbert identifies himself with Zoe's canary. Observing the captured bird in its cage in the backyard, Norbert feels sorry for "the poor boy," who, Norbert projects, is pining for freedom. Unsurprisingly Norbert goes over to notice "a resemblance between him and the canary": "He hadn't grown up in nature's freedom, but already with his birth had been hedged between bars in terms of education and predestination." But Norbert realizes "there was one aspect in which he differed from the canary quite advantageously," and that is that he, Norbert, was free to leave his cage whenever he wanted to.[11] A little later Norbert leaves Germany for Italy, where the rest of the story takes place. It is probably no coincidence that canaries are birds from the south (the Canary Islands, Madeira, and the Azores). This southernness of the bird is all too literally contrasted with Norbert's name, derived from the Old High German *nord* (north). However, Norbert and the canary are not exactly contraries' rather the canary too works as a figure of mediation, an instance of both similarity and difference. For Norbert the canary becomes an emotional catalyst that gives him occasion to realize his desires.

Still the canary is more overdetermined than being only a medium for Norbert's desire or for the sorrows of young Werther: It seems as if this bird were singing along not only with Goethe's frivolous canary but with a whole flock of exotic birds. Emma Barker and Barbara Vinken each have shown that there is "a long tradition of using birds as sexual symbols."[12] This is especially true for seventeenth-century Dutch painting and more generally for eighteenth-century French art, where the dead bird tends to appear as a symbol of seduction and lost virginity, most famously in Greuze's tableau *A Young Girl Weeping over Her Dead Bird* (1765). In *Gradiva* the happy climax of the canary's midwife function for Norbert's life of affects culminates in the moment in which "Norbert the Canary" goes south and manages to do what poor Werther can only imagine: becoming the animal that makes bestial love to the girl.

Perhaps it looks as if I am trying to pull rabbits out of hats. But although the next animal that I would like to introduce in closing as a possible precursor of Jensen's animals is a furry one, it is a creature of yet a different kind: the *Venus in Furs*. This might be surprising because Sacher-Masoch's story is anything but prudish or implicit. Other than Jensen's story, it leaves hardly any space for uncertainty, and it had to pay for this lack of flirtation. But *Venus in Furs* nevertheless seems to model or mediate Jensen's fantasy piece insofar as it is another story of a man who falls in love with a statue that comes alive, another story that moves to Italy as the place of actualized passions, another story that is inhabited by animals—bears, hyenas, hounds—another story of a young woman, a "domina,"[13] who uses more or less sadistic methods of pretending in order to cure her lover. Another text, finally, that borrows heavily from Goethe, the notorious flirt, in the form of quotations such as this: "Thou sensual, supersensual libertine, / A little girl can lead thee by the nose."[14]

NOTES

"ALMOST NOTHING; ALMOST EVERYTHING"

1. The "dialogical" Platonic trajectory of flirtation, which finds its privileged descendants in Enlightenment Romantic salon culture, seems distinct from the modern, urban figuration of flirtation as fleeting encounter.

2. For a rigorous account of the tradition of the thought-image (*Denk-bild*), including the question of the place of Simmel's writing within the constellation of Benjamin, Bloch, Kracauer, and Adorno, see Gerhard Richter, *Thought-Images: Frankfurt School Writers' Reflections from Damaged Life* (Stanford: Stanford University Press, 2007).

3. Georg Simmel, "Flirtation," in *On Women, Sexuality, and Love*, translated and introduction by Guy Oakes (New Haven: Yale University Press, 1984), 133–52.

4. Ibid., 144. For "purposiveness without purpose," see Immanuel Kant, *Critique of the Power of Judgement*, 1790, translated by Paul Guyer and Eric Matthews (Cambridge, U.K.: Cambridge University Press, 2000).

5. Ernst Bloch, "Pippa Passes," 1969, in *Traces*, translated by Anthony A. Nassar (Stanford: Stanford University Press, 2006), 59–61.

6. Ibid., 59.

7. Ibid., 60.

8. Ibid.

9. Ibid., 61.

10. Adam Phillips, *On Flirtation: Psychoanalytic Essays on the Uncommitted Life* (Cambridge, Mass.: Harvard University Press, 1994), 12.

11. In the field of literary studies itself, the most significant work is Richard Kaye's *The Flirt's Tragedy: Desire Without End in Victorian and*

Edwardian Fiction (Charlottesville: Virginia University Press, 2002), which offers a comprehensive analysis of flirtation in the nineteenth- and early twentieth-century novel. Kaye reads flirtation as a formal feature—concentrating on the temporal aspect of deferral for the novel—as well as a political moment, "a dissident gesture." Though we have learned much from Kaye's work, our project is broader in scope, covering a wider range of periods, genres, and national literary traditions. Perhaps more important and especially in distinction from Kaye's, our project is unabashedly speculative, taking flirtation as an object of general theoretical interest rather than as a period artifact or an object of strictly genealogical investigation.

12. Phillips, *On Flirtation*, xii.

13. Ibid., xxiii.

14. Ibid., xvii.

15. Roland Barthes, *A Lover's Discourse: Fragments*, 1977, translated by Richard Howard (New York: Hill and Wang, 1996), 4.

16. Ibid., 3.

17. Stanley Cavell, *Pursuits of Happiness* (Cambridge, Mass.: Harvard University Press, 1981), 7.

18. Ibid., 86.

19. It should be noted in passing that Cavell tends to read the analogy between the conversations in the films and philosophical conversation in only one direction. His intervention is to demonstrate the philosophical significance of the comedy of remarriage, but the amorous conversations of his films seem to be treated as a special case of philosophical-critical conversation rather than its paradigm, thus shielding the philosopher from a full engagement with the affective (libidinal, gendered) dimensions of the philosophical enunciation. In this regard the *Symposium* remains more radical; in Cavell no Alcibiades bursts upon the scene.

20. Cavell, *Pursuits of Happiness*, 88.

21. In this regard it is telling that Cavell, like Simmel, cites the Kantian formula of "purposefulness without purpose" but, unlike Simmel, imagines this as the "achievement" of the constituted couple; for Cavell "purposefulness without purpose" seems to presuppose the teleology of the couple (ibid., 89).

22. Niklas Luhmann, *Liebe als Passion: Zur Codierung von Intimität* (Frankfurt: Suhrkamp, 1982); Niklas Luhmann, *Love as Passion: The*

Codification of Intimacy, translated by Jeremy Gaines and Doris L. Jones (Cambridge, U.K.: Polity Press, 1986).

23. Ibid., 18–33.

24. Ibid., 28.

25. Ibid., 18.

26. Luhmann's analysis of the paradoxical "communication of the incommunicable" (ibid., 128) only underscores the degree to which communication forms the ultimate horizon of his thinking on love and literature alike.

INTERLUDE. BARELY COVERED BANTER

1. *Double Indemnity*, directed by Billy Wilder, 1944. There is an abundance of writing on the film; see, for instance, Joan Copjec, "The Phenomenal Nonphenomenal: Private Space in Film Noir," in *Shades of Noir* (London: Verso, 1993), 167–98; James Naremore, "Straight-Down-the-Line: Making and Remaking *Double Indemnity*," *Film Comment* 32.1 (1996): 22–31; Elisabeth Bronfen, "Femme Fatale: Negotiations of Tragic Desire," *New Literary History* 35.1 (2004): 103–16; Hugh S. Manon, "Some Like It Cold: Fetishism in Billy Wilder's *Double Indemnity*," *Cinema Journal* 44.4 (2005): 18–43.

2. James Cain, *Double Indemnity* (New York: Knopf, 1943).

3. Stanley Cavell, *Pursuits of Happiness* (Cambridge, Mass.: Harvard University Press, 1981). The films discussed by Cavell were produced between 1934 and 1949; *Double Indemnity*, in other words, is very much the contemporary of the comedy of remarriage.

4. Ibid., 88.

5. Ibid., 86.

6. For a philosophical account of indemnification, see Jacques Derrida, "Faith and Knowledge," translated by Samuel Weber, in *Acts of Religion*, edited by Gil Anidjar (New York: Routledge 2002), 40–101.

7. Georg Simmel, "Flirtation," in *Georg Simmel: On Women, Sexuality, and Love*, translated by Guy Oakes (New Haven: Yale University Press, 1984), 143; Georg Simmel, "Die Koketterie," in *Philosophische Kultur* (Leipzig: Klinkhardt, 1911), 90.

8. Simmel, "Flirtation," 145; Simmel, "Die Koketterie," 92.

9. In his extremely insightful 1998 review of the film, Roger Ebert touches indirectly on this question: "On their third meeting, after a lot of

aggressive wordplay, they agree to kill the husband and collect the money. I guess they also make love; in 1944 movies you can't be sure, but if they do, it's only the once." See Roger Ebert, "*Double Indemnity* Movie Review," *Chicago Sun Times*, December 20, 1998, archived at http://www.rogerebert.com/reviews/great-movie-double-indemnity-1944, accessed March 11, 2014.

10. As an editor I was able to profit from the other contributions to the volume. On flirtation and death, see Hamilton's essay and Anderson's.

11. On the relation of the Kantian formula of "purposiveness without purpose" to flirtation, see Simmel, as well as Fleming (this volume).

12. On turning away from the object of flirtation, see Simmel, "Flirtation," 135–83; Fleming (this volume).

13. This is a variant on the figure of prosopopoeia, "the giving of a mask or face"; for a classic account of prosopopoeia, see Paul de Man, "Autobiography as De-Facement," in *The Rhetoric of Romanticism* (New York: Columbia University Press, 1984), 67–82. For a related argument on the "play with the mask," see Werner Hamacher, "(The End of Art with the Mask)," translated by Kelly Barry, in *Hegel after Derrida*, edited by Stuart Barnett (London: Routledge, 1998), 105–30.

14. On allusion and intertextuality as flirtation, see Nagel, "Doing It as the Beasts Did" (this volume).

15. *The Philadelphia Story*, directed by George Cukor, 1940. For Cavell's treatment of *The Philadelphia Story*, see "The Importance of Importance: *The Philadelphia Story*," in *Pursuits of Happiness*, 134–60. As a number of people have pointed out, the mention of *The Philadelphia Story* is, taken literally, an anachronism: *Double Indemnity* takes place in 1938, one year before the Broadway production of *The Philadelphia Story* and two years before the film version. See, for instance, http://www.slipups.com/items/35949.html, accessed March 11, 2014.

16. The double "F" of course also has other, more untoward associations. Interestingly the hero of Cain's *Double Indemnity* is Walter *Huff*; the shift from "Huff" to "Neff" is enigmatic, to say the least, but the continuity between the two names affirms the generic demand for a monosyllabic name with a harsh consonantal ending.

THE ART OF FLIRTATION

1. Sigmund Freud, "Thoughts for the Times on War and Death," in *The Standard Edition of the Complete Psychological Works of Sigmund Freud*, 24 vols., translated and edited by James Strachey (London: Hogarth Press, 1981), 14: 291. Translations silently modified.

2. Ibid.

3. Ibid.

4. Georg Simmel, "The Sociology of Sociability," translated by E. C. Hughes, *American Journal of Sociology* 55.3 (1949): 254. This essay was initially delivered as a lecture in 1910 and published in 1911. Hereafter I will simply refer to it as "Sociability" and may silently modify the translation throughout.

5. Richard A. Kaye argues the opposite with respect to Freud: "Freud grasped that flirtation is less a subspecies of romantic desire than an utterly separate . . . experience." *The Flirt's Tragedy: Desire Without End in Victorian and Edwardian Fiction* (Charlottesville: University of Virginia Press, 2002), 31. Freud's metaphor, however, implies that an affair and a flirt play the same game with the same rules (poker); the former is in for big stakes (life and death, pleasure and loss) and the latter "just for fun." I agree nevertheless with Kaye's overall assessment of coquetry: "Flirtation is not simply another form of eros" (18) and "Flirtation is a distinct, overlooked category encompassing its own rules and dynamics" (21). Responding to Freud with an implicit critique, Adam Phillips succinctly states, "Flirting may not be a poor way of doing something better, but a different way of doing something else." *On Flirtation: Psychoanalytic Essays on the Uncommitted Life* (Cambridge, Mass.: Harvard University Press, 1994), xxii.

6. Simmel, "Sociability," 255.

7. Ibid., 259.

8. For a brief overview of the relation between flirtation and coquetry in the eighteenth- and nineteenth-century European context, including attempts to differentiate them, see Kaye's introduction to *The Flirt's Tragedy*, especially 21–26.

9. See, for example, Guy Oakes's introduction to *Georg Simmel: On Women, Sexuality, and Love* (New Haven: Yale University Press, 1984), 3–62. Anne Witz argues that one cannot simply extract the "good" parts of Simmel's writings on modernity with respect to gender and leave the "bad"

ones behind; rather the bad parts have to be read as symptomatic of
Simmel's philosophy as a whole, which produces an ontology of gender
that in turn shapes his sociological imagination. The result for Witz is a
"deep ontology of gender" that consigns "woman to the metaphysical
wastelands of his philosophical imagination whilst releasing man into the
more fertile and productive workings of the sociological imagination."
"Georg Simmel and the Masculinity of Modernity," *Journal of Classical
Sociology* 1.3 (2001): 355.

10. Kaye nicely encapsulates both the necessity and the difficulty of
distinguishing flirtation from seduction by describing flirtation as "seductive behavior without seduction" (*The Flirt's Tragedy*, 4).

11. See Susan Laxton, "From Judgment to Process: The Modern Ludic
Field," in *From Diversion to Subversion: Games, Play, and Twentieth-
century Art*, edited by David Getsy (University Park: Penn State University
Press, 2011), 19.

12. Simmel, "Sociability," 258.

13. See Georg Simmel, "Flirtation," in *Georg Simmel: On Women,
Sexuality, and Love*, 145. Simmel's engagement with the topic goes back to
his 1890 "The Psychology of Women" ("Zur Psychologie der Frauen").
Simmel published a version of the flirtation essay in 1909 with the title "The
Psychology of Flirtation" ("Die Psychologie der Koketterie") and another
version in 1923 simply as "Flirtation," which is the basis of Oakes's translation. Translations from this essay may be silently modified throughout.

14. Immanuel Kant, *Critique of the Power of Judgment*, edited and
translated by Paul Guyer and Eric Matthews (Cambridge, U.K.: Cambridge
University Press, 2000), §3, 92.

15. Simmel, "Flirtation," 144.

16. Simmel, "Sociability," 255.

17. See Niklas Luhmann, *Love as Passion: The Codification of Intimacy*,
translated by Jeremy Gaines and Doris Jones (Stanford: Stanford University
Press, 1998). On coquetry, see especially 50, 125, 211; Roland Barthes, *A
Lover's Discourse: Fragments*, translated by Richard Howard, 9th ed.
(New York: Hill and Wang, 1987).

18. Simmel, "Flirtation," 134–35.

19. Note that the *Grimmsches Wörterbuch* derives the etymology of
Beispiel not from *spielen* (play) but from *fabula*: "BEISPIEL, *n. fabula*,

exemplum, für beispell, *denn mit* spiel *ludus hat das wort nichts zu schaffen, es stammt aus* spell *sermo, narratio, ahd.* spel *gen.* spelles (GRAFF 6, 333), *ags.* spell, *altn.* spiall, *goth.* spill, *deren aller doppeltes* L *sich von dem einfachen in* spil *ludus wesentlich scheidet. wie* fabula."

20. On "Bei-Spiel" or "By-play," see Andrej Warminski, *Readings in Interpretation: Hölderlin, Hegel, Heidegger* (Minneapolis: University of Minnesota Press, 1987), especially chapter 5, "Pre-positional By-play."

21. Simmel, "Flirtation," 135.

22. I am expanding and elaborating on Simmel's own mock quotation to express the scene. Simmel describes the unspoken of playing with the dog, flower, and so on as follows: " 'It is not you that interests me, but rather these things here.' And yet at the same time: 'This is a game I'm playing for your benefit. It is because of my interest in you that I turn to these other things' " ("Flirtation," 135).

23. Kaye, *The Flirt's Tragedy*, 23. The flirtatious glance may therefore only seem to say it all; sometimes the attention and affection given to a dog may actually be for the dog and not some mediated form of attention to a third, to "you," a point that will be discussed in the next thesis.

24. Simmel makes this duality explicit in describing coquetry that has not yet reached its full, playful, sociable form of mutuality as follows: "When a woman flirts 'with' one man in order to flirt with another who is the actual object of her intentions, the double meaning of the word 'with' is profoundly revealed" ("Flirtation," 136). This double sense incorporates both an instrumentality and a partnership in correlation. The ideal of flirtation, however, is when this duality occurs "with" one and the same person.

25. Simmel, "Sociability," 258. See "The pleasure of the individual is always contingent upon the joy of others; here, by definition, no one can have his satisfaction at the cost of contrary experience on the part of others" (257).

26. Ibid., 257.

27. Simmel, "Flirtation," 144.

28. See Kaye's chess metaphor, which follows Simmel's essential description of flirtation as a game or art: "Two people engaged in a flirtation are closer to players involved in an explicitly coded game, such as chess, than ordinary users of language" (*The Flirt's Tragedy*, 34).

29. It can do so because all forms of sociability, including coquetry, exclude to a certain degree the personal (see Simmel, "Sociability," 256); with this exclusion one gains what Simmel describes as the ability to "abandon [oneself] to the impersonal freedom of the mask" (256). In flirtation one doesn't reveal but plays oneself; in a sense one flirts with oneself, with the persona of a self, while flirting with another person.

30. As a general mode of conduct, flirtation doesn't master indecision in life (i.e., doesn't turn it into a decision, whether as refusal or consent) but rather crystallizes nondecision into "a thoroughly positive way of acting. Although its does not make a virtue of this necessity, it does make it into a pleasure" (Simmel, "Flirtation," 151).

31. Ibid., 136. Roland Barthes writes in similar terms regarding the erotic photograph and its aesthetics of nonshowing: "The erotic photograph, on the contrary (and this is its very condition), does not make the sexual organs into a central object; it may very well not show them at all; it takes the spectator outside its frame, and it is there that I animate this photograph and that it animates me." *Camera Lucida: Reflections on Photography*, translated by Richard Howard (London: Fontana Paperbacks, 1984), 59.

32. Simmel, "Flirtation," 135.

33. Carl Schmitt, *Political Theology: Four Chapters on the Concept of Sovereignty*, translated by George Schwab (Chicago: University of Chicago Press, 2005), 5.

34. Simmel, "Flirtation," 136.

35. Herbert Marcuse, *One Dimensional Man*, 2nd edition (1964; Boston: Beacon Press, 1991), 4.

36. Simmel, "Flirtation," 144.

37. T. W. Adorno, *Aesthetic Theory*, translated by Robert Hullot-Kenner (Minneapolis: University of Minnesota Press, 1997), 311. See T. W. Adorno and Max Horkheimer, *Dialectic of Enlightenment: Philosophical Fragments*, translated by Edmund Jephcott (Stanford: Stanford University Press, 2007), 111.

38. Simmel, "Flirtation," 142.

39. Laxton, "From Judgment to Process," 23.

40. Simmel, "Sociability," 258.

41. Ibid., 260.

42. Dante, *Inferno*, canto V, 138.

43. Simmel, "Flirtation," 145.

44. Ibid., 136.

45. Ibid.

46. "It is women lacking fantasy who inflame fantasy the most." T. W. Adorno, *Minima Moralia: Reflections on a Damaged Life*, translated by E. F. H. Jephcott (London: Verso, 2005), 169, §108. Translation modified.

47. Timothy Perper, "Will She or Won't She: The Dynamics of Flirtation on Western Philosophy," *Sexuality & Culture* 14 (2010): 39. On flirtation as essentially a mode of potentiality, see Perper: "It [flirtation] promises not a kiss, but the *potential* of a kiss" (38).

48. Adorno, *Aesthetic Theory*, 11.

"THE DOUBLE-SENSE OF THE 'WITH' "

1. Martin Heidegger, *Being and Time*, 1962, translated by John Macquarrie and Edward Robinson (Oxford: Blackwell, 2001), 149–68; Jean-Luc Nancy, *Being Singular Plural*, translated by Anne O'Byrne and Robert Richardson (Stanford: Stanford University Press, 2000), 1–100

2. Georg Simmel, "On Flirtation," in *Georg Simmel: On Women, Sexuality, and Love*, translated by Guy Oakes (New Haven: Yale University Press, 1984), 136; Georg Simmel, "Die Koketterie," in *Philosophische Kultur* (Leipzig: Klinkhardt, 1911), 84.

3. For an excellent treatment of questions of reciprocity, instrumentality, and pleasure, to which I am indebted throughout, see Jacques Lezra, "A Sadean Community," in *Wild Materialism* (New York: Fordham University Press, 2010), 150–72.

4. See Immanuel Kant, *Groundwork of the Metaphysics of Morals*, translated by Mary J. Gregor, introduction by Christine Korsgard (Cambridge, U.K.: Cambridge University Press, 1998).

5. Simmel, "On Flirtation," 136; Simmel, "Die Koketterie," 84.

6. Unsurprisingly the question of same-sex flirtation does not come up explicitly in Simmel's essay; it would be interesting to pursue this question further, particularly in relation to one of Simmel's privileged intertexts, namely Plato's *Symposium*.

7. Though this response essay cannot explore this question in detail, perhaps this is also the place to note that the substantive *die Kokette* is queer

in another sense, in that it is an interlingual French-German hybrid; this strangeness is only accented by the hybrid verbalization of "kokettieren mit."

8. Simmel, "On Flirtation," 133; Simmel, "Die Koketterie," 81.

9. *Plato's Symposium*, translated and with introduction and notes by Alexander Nehamas and Paul Woodruff (Indianapolis: Hackett, 1987), 204A, 49.

10. Ibid., 204B, 49.

11. Simmel, "On Flirtation," 133–34; Simmel, "Die Koketterie," 81–82.

12. Here it is worth quoting at length Jean-Luc Nancy's "Shattered Love," 1986, in *The Inoperative Community*, edited by Peter Connor, introduction by Christopher Fynsk (Minneapolis: University Press of Minnesota, 2004), 85: "Although the *Symposium* speaks of love, it also does more than that; it opens thought to love as to its own essence. This is why this dialogue is more than any other the dialogue of Plato's generosity: here he invites orators or thinkers and offers them a speech tempered altogether differently from the speech of the interlocutors of Socrates. The scene itself, the gaiety or the joy that traverses it, attests to a consideration that is unique in Plato (to such a degree, at least)—consideration for others, as well as for the object of discourse. All the different kinds of loves are welcomes in the *Symposium*; there is discussion, but there is no exclusion."

13. Simmel, "On Flirtation," 144, 145; Simmel, "Die Koketterie," 91, 92.

14. Georg Simmel, "'Introduction' to Philosophical Culture," in *Simmel on Culture: Selected Writings*, edited by David Frisby and Mike Featherstone (London: Sage, 2000), 33; Georg Simmel, "Einleitung," in *Philosophische Kultur* (Leipzig: Klinkhardt, 1911), 7.

RHETORIC'S FLIRTATION WITH LITERATURE,
FROM GORGIAS TO ARISTOTLE

1. See Eduard Norden, *Die antike Kunstprosa vom VI. Jahrhundert vor Christus bis in die Zeit der Renaissance* (Leipzig: Teubner, 1898).

2. For text and commentary see Gorgias of Leontini, *Encomio di Elena*, edited by Luca Càffaro (Florence: Aletheia, 1997), 18–19; the English translation follows "The Encomium of Helen by Gorgias of Leontini," translated by Brian R. Donovan, 1999, http://www.bemidjistate.edu /academics/departments/english/Donovan/helen.html, accessed February 25, 2012.

3. Thucydides, *History of the Peloponnesian War*, translated by Rex Warner, introduction by M. I. Finley (Harmondsworth, U.K.: Penguin Books, 1972), book 2, chap. 3, 143–51.

4. See Vincenz Buchheit, *Untersuchungen zur Theorie des Genos Epideiktikon von Gorgias bis Aristoteles* (München: Max Huber Verlag, 1960); Laurent Pernot, *Le rhétorique de l'éloge dans le monde gréco-romain* (Paris: Institut des Etudes Augustiniennes, 1993).

5. Thucydides, *History*, 151 (translation modified).

6. Gorgias, "The Encomium of Helen," 21; Gorgias, *Encomio di Elena*, 34–35.

7. Gorgias, "The Encomium of Helen," 6; Gorgias, *Encomio di Elena*, 22–23.

8. Gorgias, "The Encomium of Helen," 13; Gorgias, *Encomio di Elena*, 28–29.

9. Gorgias, "The Encomium of Helen," 9; Gorgias, *Encomio di Elena*, 24–25.

10. See Buchheit, *Untersuchungen zur Theorie des Genos Epideiktikon*, n3.

11. Ernst Robert Curtius, *Europäische Literatur und lateinisches Mittelalter*, 2nd edition (Bern: Francke, 1954), 74, 164; Ernst Robert Curtius, *European Literature and the Latin Middle Ages*, translated by W. R. Trask (1990; Princeton: Princeton University Press, 2013), 65, 155.

12. Martin Heidegger, *Basic Concepts of Aristotelian Philosophy*, translated by R. D. Metcalf and M. B. Tanzer (Bloomington: Indiana University Press, 2009).

13. Aristotle, *Art of Rhetoric*, translated by J. H. Freese (Cambridge, Mass.: Harvard University Press, 1994), books 1 and 2. For a more detailed presentation of the argument that further connects the affects in court to the motives of action in the world or wrongdoing, see Rüdiger Campe, "An Outline for a Critical History of *Fürsprache: Synegoria* and Advocacy," *Deutsche Vierteljahrsschrift* 82 (2008): 355–81.

14. Richard Lockwood, *The Reader's Figure: Epideictic Rhetoric in Plato, Aristotle, Bossuet, Racine and Pascal* (Geneva: Droz, 1996).

15. Aristotle, *Art of Rhetoric* 1358b (I. 2).

16. Ibid. The passage illustrates the eccentricity and yet integrative position of the epideictic nicely: First, Aristotle juxtaposes judge (in

juridical and political speech) with spectator (in epideictic speech). This shows the divide between the two institutional genres and the one quasi-institutional genre. Then, however, he reinterprets the spectator in terms of what he is not: a judge. A judge can be a judge only about the *dynamis* of speaker or speech, his or its potentiality.

17. Aristotle, *The Art of Rhetoric*, 1413b (III.12).

18. Ibid., 1414a (III.12).

19. See Lockwood, *The Reader's Figure*, n14.

20. See Richard Graff, "Reading and the 'Written Style' in Aristotle's Rhetoric," *Rhetoric Society Quarterly* 31 (2001): 19–44.

21. Quintilian, *The Orator's Education*, translated by Donald A. Russell (Cambridge, Mass.: Harvard University Press, 2001), 8.4.21.

PLAYING WITH YOURSELF

1. See David Wellbery, "Scheinvorgang: *Kafkas* Das Schweigen der Sirenen," in *Seiltänzer des Paradoxalen: Aufsätze zur ästhetischen Wissenschaft* (München: Carl Hanser Verlag, 207), 177–95.

2. Franz Kafka, "The Silence of the Sirens," in *The Complete Stories*, edited by Nahum N. Glatzer (New York: Schocken 1971), 431. German original: "Sie aber, schöner als jemals, streckten und drehten sich, ließen das schaurige Haar offen im Wind wehn, spannten die Krallen frei auf den Felsen, sie wollten nicht mehr verführen, nur noch den Abglanz vom großen Augenpaar des Odysseus wollten sie solange als möglich erhaschen." Franz Kafka, *Nachgelassene Schriften und Fragmente*, vol. 2, KA, 41.

3. See George Spencer Brown, *Laws of Form* (London: Allen & Unwin)1969); Niklas Luhmann, *Die Wissenschaft der Gesellschaft* (Frankfurt/Main: Suhrkamp, 1990); Niklas Luhmann, "Observing Reentries," *Graduate Faculty Philosophy Journal* 16.2 (1993): 485–98.

4. Gorgias, "Encomium of Helen," in *The Norton Anthology of Theory and Criticism*, edited by Vincent B. Leitch et al. (New York: Norton, 2001), 33.

5. See Elisabeth Strowick, *Sprechende Körper—Poetik der Ansteckung: Performativa in Literatur und Rhetorik* (München: Fink, 2009); Wolfram Groddeck, *Reden über Rhetorik: Zu einer Stilistik des Lesens* (Basel: Stroemfeld/Nexus, 1995).

6. Gorgias, "Encomium of Helen," 33.

7. See Strowick, *Sprechende Körper*, 58–59.

8. Niklas Luhmann, *Love as Passion: The Codification of Intimacy*, translated by Jeremy Gaines and Doris L. Jones (Cambridge, U.K.: Polity Press, 1986), 31–32.

9. Ibid., 11.

INTERLUDE. STAGING APPEAL, PERFORMING AMBIVALENCE

1. Here Butler is expanding on Esther Newton's *Mother Camp: Impersonations in America* (Chicago: University of Chicago Press, 1972), in particular Newton's description of impersonation as a "double inversion." It is similarly useful alongside flirtation—especially with regard to the following essays—to consider how "drag fully subverts the notion of inner and outer psychic space." Flirtation troubles the simple relations of inner and outer, particularly as division between (inner) intent and (outer) expression (Butler, *Gender Trouble*, 187).

2. And of course one can also change one's mind! What begins as a flirtation could turn into seduction, or an apparent seduction could be rerouted, reconceived as mere flirtation to save face.

LIFE IS A FLIRTATION

1. Thomas Mann, *Confessions of Felix Krull, Confidence Man*, translated by Denver Lindley (New York: Knopf, 1955), 44 (hereafter abbreviated as C); Thomas Mann, *Bekenntnisse des Hochstaplers Felix Krull: Große kommentierte Frankfurter Ausgabe: Werke–Briefe–Tagebücher* (Frankfurt/Main: S. Fischer, 2012), 58 (hereafter abbreviated as B).

2. "Dichte Reihen von Schinken und Würsten, . . . weisse, ockergelbe, rote und schwarze, solche, die prall und rund waren wie Kugeln, sowie lange, knotige, strickartige, verdunkelten das Gewölbe. Blechbüchsen und Konserven, Kakao und Tee, bunte Gläser mit Marmeladen, Honig und Eingemachtem, schlanke und bauchige Flaschen mit Likören und Punschessenzen füllten die Wandborde vom Fussboden bis zur Decke. In den gläsernen Schaukästen des Ladentisches boten sich geräucherte Fische, Makrelen, Neunaugen, Flundern und Aale auf Tellern und Schüsseln dem Genusse dar. . . . Artischocken, Bündel von grünen Spargeln, Häufchen von Trüffeln, kostbare kleine Leberwürste in Stanniol waren wie in

prahlerischem Überfluss dazwischen verteilt, und auf Nebentischen
standen offene Blechbüchsen voll feiner Biskuits, waren braun glänzende
Honigkuchen kreuzweise übereinandergeschichtet, erhoben sich . . .
Glasschalen mit Dessertbonbons und überzuckerten Früchten"
(B 54–55).

3. Jacques Lacan, *The Four Fundamental Concepts of Psycho-Analysis*,
edited by Jacques-Alain Miller, translated by Alan Sheridan (New York:
Norton, 1981), 115.

4. "[Lockend-belehrende] Auslagen der Welt"(B 95).

5. "Feinere[n], köstlichere[n], verflüchtigtere[n] Arten der Genugtuung"
(B 63).

6. "Ich hatte die Natur verbessert, einen Traum verwirklicht,—und wer
je aus dem Nichts, aus der . . . Phantasie, unter kühner Einsetzung seiner
Person eine zwingende, wirksame Wirklichkeit zu schaffen vermochte, der
kennt die . . . träumerische Zufriedenheit, mit der ich damals von meiner
Schöpfung ausruhte" (B 49).

7. "Es war nichts, nur war es reizend" (B 96).

8. Sigmund Freud, "Negation," in *The Standard Edition of the Complete
Psychological Works of Sigmund Freud* (London: Hogarth Press, 1961), 19:
238. "Die äußeren Reize verkostet, um sich nach jedem solchen tastenden
Vorstoß wieder zurückzuziehen." Sigmund Freud, "Die Verneinung,"
Studienausgabe (Frankfurt/Main: Fischer, 1975), 3: 376.

9. Sigmund Freud, "A Note upon the 'Mystic Writing-Pad,' " in *The
Standard Edition*, 19: 231.

10. "Wie doch das erfinderische Leben die Träume unserer Kindheit
zu verwirklichen—sie gleichsam aus Nebelzustand in den der Festigkeit
zu überführen weiss! Hatte ich die Reize des Inkognitos, die ich jetzt
kostete, indem ich noch eine kleine Weile mein dienendes Handwerk
weiterbetrieb, nicht phantasieweise schon als Knabe vorweggenommen,
ohne dass sonst irgend jemand von meiner Prinzlichkeit eine Ahnung
hatte? Ein so lustiges wie süsses Kinderspiel. Jetzt war es Wirklichkeit
geworden" (B 291).

11. "Indem ich die Feder ergreife, um in völliger Muße und
Zurückgezogenheit—gesund übrigens, wenn auch müde, sehr müde (so
dass ich wohl nur in kleinen Etappen und unter häufigem Ausruhen werde
vorwärtsschreiten können), indem ich mich also anschicke, meine

Geständnisse in der sauberen und gefälligen Handschrift, die mir eigen ist, dem geduldigen Papier anzuvertrauen, beschleicht mich das flüchtige Bedenken, ob ich diesem geistigen Unternehmen nach Vorbildung und Schule denn auch gewachsen bin" (B 9).

12. Freud, "A Note upon the 'Mystic Writing-Pad,' " 19: 232.

13. Jacques Derrida, "Freud and the Scene of Writing," translated by Jeffrey Mehlman, in "French Freud: Structural Studies in Psychoanalysis," special edition of *Yale French Studies* 48 (1972): 112. See also: Jacques Derrida, "Freud et la scène de l'écriture," in *L'écriture et la différence.* (Paris: Éditions du Seuil: 1967), 334.

14. "—gesund übrigens, wenn auch müde, sehr müde (so dass ich wohl nur in kleinen Etappen und unter häufigem Ausruhen werde vorwärtsschreiten können)" (B 9).

15. See Manfred von Roncador and Wolfram Bublitz, "Abschweifungen," in *Partikeln der deutschen Sprache*, edited by Harald Weydt (Berlin: de Gruyter, 1979), 287.

16. "Zu dem schon Vorhandenen noch hinzu kommend." Johann August Eberhard, Johann Gebhard Ehrenreich Maass, and Johann Gottfried Gruber, *Deutsche Synonymik*, vol. 2: *K–Z*, 4th ed. (Leipzig: Johann Ambrosius Barth, 1853), 408.

17. "What is still to be added is what is left-over from the thing being discussed in what has been said already [*dasz das noch hinzuzusetzende dasjenige sey, was das bereits gesetzte von der in rede stehenden Sache noch übrig gelassen habe*] (Maass, et al, *Synonymik*, 5: 185), quoted after Jacob Grimm and Wilhelm Grimm, *Deutsches Wörterbuch* (Leipzig: Hirzel, 1936), 704.

18. Jacques Derrida, "The Double Session," in *Dissemination*, translated by Barbara Johnson (Chicago: University of Chicago Press, 1988), 219, 191, 206, 208.

19. See also Roland Barthes, "The Reality Effect," in *The Rustle of Language*, translated by Richard Howard (Oxford: Blackwell, 1986), 141–48.

20. Jacques Derrida, *Spurs: Nietzsche's Styles / Éperons: Les Styles de Nietzsche*, translated by Barbara Harlow (Chicago: University of Chicago Press, 1981), 47.

21. Derrida, "The Double Session," 195.

22. "Die untere Hälfte des E nämlich lud weit zu gefälligem Schwunge aus, in dessen offenen Schoss die kurze Silbe das Nachnamens sauber eingetragen wurde. Von oben her aber den u-Haken zum Anlass und Ausgang nehmend und alles von vorn umfassend, gesellte sich ein zweiter Schnörkel hinzu, welcher den E-Schwung zweimal schnitt, und gleich diesem von Zierpunkten flankiert, in zügiger S-Form nach unten verlief" (B 43).

23. Derrida, "The Double Session," 194.

24. Samuel Weber, *Theatricality as Medium* (New York: Fordham University Press, 2004), 15.

25. See also Rosalind E. Krauss, "The Blink of an Eye," in *The States of "Theory": History, Art, and Critical Discourse*, edited by David Carroll (New York: Columbia University Press, 1990), 175–99.

THE "IRREDUCIBLY DOUBLED STROKE"

1. In addition to citing J. L. Austin's *How to Do Things with Words* (Cambridge, Mass.: Harvard University Press, 1962) directly over the course of this essay, I will also make frequent direct and oblique reference to both Stanley Cavell's "Must We Mean What We Say?" *Must we mean what we say?* (Cambridge, Mass.: Cambridge University Press, 2002) and Hent de Vries's essay "Must We (NOT) Mean What We Say? Seriousness and Sincerity in the Work of J. L. Austin and Stanley Cavell," in *The Rhetoric of Sincerity*, edited by Ernst Van Alpen et al. (Stanford: Stanford University Press, 2009), which also cites liberally from both Austin and Cavell. There is significant and necessary overlap among them—and all of these texts, de Vries's essay in particular, are the intended referents.

2. Although Austin himself revises his theory beyond the provisional overlapping categories (descriptive, constative, and performative), this framework captures more clearly the persistent ambivalence in one's experience of meaning in precisely the way that I emphasize here. Though I will briefly address this in terms of the distinctions that Austin himself settled on (locutionary-illocutionary acts), it will be evident why this earlier system illuminates the flirtation more accurately.

3. As Cavell and later de Vries have variously pointed out, there need not be anything heretical in the use of Derrida as a springboard for what will be a reading that relies heavily on Austin's speech act theory. Though I am well

aware of the debate between (among?) them, I do not have the space here to address how and where their theories do in fact come into conflict. If anything, I hope to contribute to the areas of discourse that, like Cavell and de Vries, illuminate the shared concerns about the stakes of language.

4. Strowick quoting Jacques Derrida, "The Double Session," *Dissemination*, translated by Barbara Johnson (Chicago: University of Chicago Press), 206, 208.

5. In this way the *Generaldirektor*'s assertion "You will be named Armand [Sie werden Armand genannt werden]" takes on that peculiar kind of rule-like yet prophetic quality that concerned Cavell, insofar as the *meaning* and *must mean* become entangled in a nebulous manner. Is he instructing Felix (just as one might say "You will wash the dishes" might be an *imperative* or a *description* of responsibilities)? Or is it also a constative as this becomes a potentially verifiable statement—Felix eventually is "named" Armand. Alternatively we might also ask whether the *Generaldirektor*'s and Felix's apparent abuse of convention might complicate the ordinary value of it; that is, the use of a statement in a context that is not exactly nonsensical but certainly presses upon the limits of practical use (and as Cavell would say, sounds "fishy") thus begs further analysis. Stanley Cavell, "Must We Mean What We Say?" *Must we mean what we say?* (Cambridge, Mass.: Cambridge University Press, 2002).

6. Austin, *How to Do Things with Words*, 109.

7. Ibid., 136.

8. Though I do not have the space to elaborate it here, I think that we can reasonably consider the utterances (those of the *Generaldirektor* as well as Felix) within what Wittgenstein calls the "language-game." Though there is a certain absurdity to these scenes, the utterances themselves nonetheless belong to the universe in which they are used and can be described, however problematically, as "meaning something coherently." That an utterance is not grammatically or conventionally "senseless" is part of Wittgenstein's strategy of drawing limit cases. We might think of these scenes similarly.

9. This is, as we suggested in the introduction to this volume, perhaps a driving force behind the play of representation and the depth of literature. See also Stanley Cavell, *The Claim of Reason: Wittgenstein, Skepticism, Morality, and Tragedy* (New York: Oxford University Press, 1979), 338.

10. Ibid., 337, emphasis mine.

11. De Vries, "Must We (NOT) Mean What We Say?," 116.

12. It is certainly worth noting that for Felix (T. Mann) "airy nothings" (*Nebelzustand*) seem to be the source of inventiveness (and arguably the closest thing to the authentic Felix), and for de Vries the "airy space of nothingness" is the material heart of the matter (ibid., 118). See Strowick, this volume.

FRILL AND FLIRTATION

1. On the onomatapoetic character of "flirt," see also John T. Hamilton, "The Luxury of Self-Destruction: Flirting with Mimesis with Roger Caillois" (this volume).

2. The title of Michel Delpech's 1971 chanson would translate into English as "For a flirt with you / I would do anything."

3. Charles Baron de Montesquieu, *The Spirit of the Laws,* translated and edited by Anne M. Cohler, Basia C. Miller, and Harold S. Stone (Cambridge, U.K.: Cambridge University Press, 1989), 311–12.

4. Ibid., 104.

5. Jean-Jacques Rousseau, *Politics and the Arts: Letter to M. D'Alembert on the Theatre,* translated by Allan Bloom (Ithaca, N.Y.: Cornell University Press, 1968), 100.

6. Ibid., 112, emphasis mine.

7. See Barbara Vinken, *Fashion—Zeitgeist: Trends and Cycles in the Fashion System* (London: Berg, 2005), 3–40.

8. See Tiqqun, *Premiers matériaux pour une Théorie de la jeune fille* (Paris: Fayard, 2001).

9. See Pierre Saint-Amand, "Terrorizing Marie-Antoinette," in *Marie-Antoinette: Writings on the Body of a Queen,* edited by Dena Goodman (New York: Routledge, 2003), 263.

10. Daniele Tamagni, *Gentlemen of Bacongo* (London: Trolley Books, 2009).

11. Alain Mabanckou, *Black Bazar* (Paris: Seuil, 2009), 44, my translation. See also the English translation: Alain Mabanckou, *Black Bazaar,* translated by Sarah Ardizzone (London: Serpent's Tail, 2012).

12. Thomas Carlyle, *Sartor Resartus: On Heroes and Hero Worship,* edited by W. H. Hudson (London: Dent, 1984), 204. By way of counterexample, one thinks of Alberta Hunter's 1961 blues song "I Got Myself a

Workin' Man." "He could win no beauty contest, and goodness knows he don't dress fine," sings Hunter of her titular "workin' man."

13. Mabanckou, *Black Bazar*, 48, my translation.

14. For the appropriation of black styles by mainstream fashion, translating Harlem to Paris already in the 1920s, see Cecil Beaton, *The Glass of Fashion* (London: Doubleday, 1954), 133–35. For the deconstructive aspect of the reappropriation in African culture, see Okwui Enwezor and Yinka Shonibare, "Of Hedonism, Masquerade, Carnivalesque and Power," in *Looking Both Ways: Art of the Contemporary African Diaspora*, edited by Laurie Ann Farell and Valentijn Byvanck (New York: Museum for African Art, 2003), 162–77.

15. Hanne Loreck, "La Sape: Eine Fallstudie zu Mode und Sichtbarkeit im postkolonialen Kontext," in *Intersektionalität und Kulturindustrie: Zum Verhältnis sozialer Kategorien und kultureller Repräsentationen*, edited by Katharina Knüttel and Martin Seeliger (Bielefeld, Germany: Transcript, 2011), 259–82.

LEARNING TO FLIRT WITH DON JUAN

1. In contrast to Lauren Shizuko Stone's argument that the flirt operates according to an ambivalent notion of sincerity and seriousness (suggesting "that perhaps the only sincerity one can count on is the sincerity of the one who doesn't actually mean it"), this essay will work with the denotative sense of the term *flirtation* as something fundamentally uncommitted and unserious. See Stone, "The 'Irreducibly Doubled Stroke," this volume.

2. Molière, *Don Juan and Other Plays*, translated by George Graveley and Ian Maclean, edited by Ian Maclean (Oxford: Oxford University Press, 1968), 36.

3. For a classic example, see Claude Reichler, *La Diabolie: La séduction, la renardie, l'écriture* (Paris: Minuit 1979).

4. Molière, *Don Juan*, 37–38.

5. Ibid., 43.

6. Ibid., 34.

7. Ibid., 43.

8. Ibid., 49.

9. Ibid., 49–50.

10. Ibid., 50, emphasis added.

11. Ibid., 74, 76.

12. Shoshana Felman, *The Literary Speech Act: Don Juan with J. L. Austin, or Seduction in Two Languages*, translated by Catherine Porter (Ithaca, N.Y.: Cornell University Press, 1983), 28.

13. Molière, *Don Juan*, 57.

14. Felman, *The Literary Speech Act*, 26–27.

15. Ibid., 27.

INTERLUDE. THREE TERRORS OF FLIRTATION

1. Thomas Mann, *Der Zauberberg* (Frankfurt/Main: Fischer, 1987), 155, my translation.

2. Joann Ellison Rodgers, "Flirting Fascination," *Psychology Today*, January 1, 1999, http://www.psychologytoday.com/articles/199901/flirting-fascination?page=3, accessed September 20, 2012.

3. Henry James, *Daisy Miller: A Study*, in *Tales of Henry James*, edited by Christof Wegelin and Henry B. Wonham, Norton Critical Edition (New York: Norton, 2003), 12.

4. Ibid., 7–8.

5. Ibid., 45.

6. Georg Simmel, *On Women, Sexuality, and Love*, edited and translated by Guy Oakes (New Haven: Yale University Press, 1984), 140.

7. Ibid., 141.

8. Jean-Paul Sartre, *Being and Nothingness*, 1942, translated by Hazel E. Barnes (New York: Philosophical Library, 1956), 323.

9. Ibid., 329.

10. Craigslist, August 6, 2013, http://www.craigslist.org/about/best/nyc/3985247459.html, accessed March 6, 2014. The ad also appeared in Chris Heller, "The Loveliest Short Story You Will Read Today Was Published on Craigslist," *Atlantic*, August 9, 2013.

11. Jean-François Lyotard, "Acinema (1973)," in *Narrative, Apparatus, Ideology. A Film Theory Reader*, edited by Philip Rosen (New York: Columbia University Press, 1986), 350–51.

THE LUXURY OF SELF-DESTRUCTION

1. Sigmund Freud, "Zeitgemässes über Krieg und Tod," 1915, in *Gesammelte Werke* (Frankfurt/M.: S. Fischer, 1959), 10: 344.

2. Plato, *Cratylus* 432 b–c, in *Plato: Complete Works*, edited by J. M. Cooper, translated by C. D. C. Reeve (Indianapolis: Hackett, 1997), 148. The Greek text is from *Platonis Opera*, vol. 1, edited by J. Burnet (Oxford: Oxford University Press, 1900).

3. Plato, *Republic* 3.395b, translated by G. M. A. Grube, in *Complete Works*, 1033.

4. *Theog.* 137ff, as quoted, in *Rep.* 377e–378a, translated by G. M. A. Grube, in *Complete Works*, 1016.

5. For further examples, see William Pressly, "The Praying Mantis in Surrealist Art," *Art Bulletin* 55 (1973): 600–615.

6. Roger Caillois, *The Edge of Surrealism: A Roger Caillois Reader*, edited by C. Frank (Durham, N.C.: Duke University Press, 2003), 91. All subsequent citations from Caillois's work are from this edition.

7. Roger Caillois, "Mimicry and Legendary Psychasthenia," in *The Edge of Surrealism*, 96–97.

8. For an extended and insightful reading, see Rosalind Krauss, "Corpus Delicti," *October* 33 (1985): 31–72.

9. *Inst. orat.* 7.3.24.

10. See Joyce Cheng, "Mask, Mimicry, Metamorphosis: Roger Caillois, Walter Benjamin, and Surrealism in the 1930s," *Modernism/modernity* 16 (2009): 61–86. On the broader ramifications for intellectual history, see Michael Weingrad, "The College of Sociology and the Institute of Social Research," *New German Critique* 84 (2001): 129–61.

11. Georges Bataille, "The Notion of Expenditure," in *Visions of Excess: Selected Writings, 1927–1939*, translated by A. Stoekl (Minneapolis: University of Minnesota Press, 1985), 116–29.

12. For further discussion, see Carlos Marroquin, *Die Religionstheorie des Collège de Sociologie: Von den irrationalen Dimensionen der Moderne* (Berlin: Parerga, 2005), 159–92.

13. Alfred de Musset, *Le Coupe et les lèvres*, 4:1, cited in Caillois, "The Praying Mantis," 78.

WARTIME LOVE AFFAIRS AND DEATHLY FLIRTATION

1. Freud as quoted and translated by Hamilton.

2. Sigmund Freud, "Zeitgemässes über Krieg und Tod," in *Gesammelte Werke* (London: Imago, 1946), 10: 344. All subsequent citations from Freud are my own translations from this edition, the one also used by Hamilton.

3. With this phrasing—a change in the structure of experience—I am thinking of Walter Benjamin, who devotes protracted attention to the impact of war on the communicability of experience in relationship to death, centrally in the following essays: "Erfahrung und Armut" (1933), "Der Erzähler" (1936), and "Über einige Motive bei Baudelaire" (1939).

4. Freud, "Zeitgemässes über Krieg und Tod," 328. For a reading of Freud's essay that also takes into consideration his later correspondence with Einstein on the question *Warum Krieg?* (1933), see Anthony Sampson, "Freud on the State, Violence, and War," *Diacritics* 35.3 (2005): 78–91.

5. See Sander L. Gilman, *Freud, Race, and Gender* (Princeton: Princeton University Press, 1993); Celia Brickman, *Aboriginal Populations in the Mind: Race and Primitivity in Psychoanalysis* (New York: Columbia University Press, 2003).

6. Freud, "Zeitgemässes über Krieg und Tod," 326.

7. On a different register, this timely Freudian conclusion recalls certain of Nietzsche's untimely (*unzeitgemäße*) insights, as in the aphoristic "Critique of the Morality of Décadence," which ends, "Dissolution of the instincts! It is all over for human beings when they become altruistic." Friedrich Nietzsche, "Raids of an Untimely Man," in *Twilight of the Idols, or, How to Philosophize with the Hammer*, translated by Richard Polt (Indianapolis: Hackett, 1997), no. 35.

8. Freud, "Zeitgemässes über Krieg und Tod," 326.

9. Ibid., 331.

10. Ibid., 339–40.

11. Ibid., 343.

12. For an extended discussion of fictional representation and theatricality in Freud's writing, further taking into account narrative aspects of dream-work and the death drive, see Samuel Weber, *The Legend of Freud* (Stanford: Stanford University Press, 2000), especially 50–66, 186–206.

13. Hamilton points primarily to the Platonic dialogue *Cratylus* and to the *Republic*.

14. For a valuable problematization of binary oppositions between strength/weakness and masculine/feminine, see Michael O'Sullivan, *Weakness: A Literary and Philosophical History* (London: Continuum, 2012), especially 1–22, 93–108.

15. "In general he [Caillois] exhibited a strong interest in nonhuman forms of creativity, in an aesthetics emancipated from human forms of subjective, rational agency—perhaps an aesthetics of flirtation" (Hamilton, this volume).

16. For additional context, see Joyce Cheng, "Mask, Mimicry, Metamorphosis: Roger Caillois, Walter Benjamin, and Surrealism in the 1930s," *Modernism/modernity* 16. 1 (2009): 61–86.

17. In Caillois's view, "at the limit, for science everything is milieu." Roger Caillois, "Mimétisme et Psychasthénie légendaire," in *Le mythe et l'homme* (Paris: Gallimard, 1938), 129n2. Translations are mine, unless quoted from Hamilton.

18. Ibid., 131. With respect to documentary evidence, Caillois's sources, already selectively interpreted, have been complicated or challenged by subsequent scientific discoveries.

19. Ibid., 141.

20. *Jenseits des Lustprinzips* was first published in 1920, five years later than *Zeitgemäßes über Krieg und Tod*, after the end of World War I.

21. Caillois, "Mimétisme et Psychasthénie légendaire," 138, emphasis added.

22. "(Ptérochroses et Phancrotérides)." Ibid., 134.

23. Ibid., 137.

BESTIALITY

1. Sigmund Freud, "Delusions and Dreams in Jensen's Gradiva," in *The Standard Edition of the Complete Psychological Works of Sigmund Freud*, vol. 9: *Jensen's "Gradiva" and Other Works*, edited by James Strachey, London: Hogarth Press, 1959, 1–96. The German of both texts is drawn from Sigmund Freud, "Der Wahn und die Träume in W. Jensens 'Gradiva,' " 1906, in *Gesammelte Werke* (London: Imago, 1993), 7: 31–123. The English of Jensen's story is from *Gradiva: A Pompeiian Fancy,* translated by Helen M. Downey (New York: Moffat, 1918).

2. Sigmund Freud, "From the History of an Infantile Neurosis," in *The Standard Edition*, vol. 17: *An Infantile Neurosis and Other Works* (London: Hogarth Press, 1917–1919), 1–124. Here is Freud's conclusion: "Scenes of observing sexual intercourse between parents at a very early age (whether they be real memories or phantasies) are as a matter of fact by no means

rarities in the analyses of neurotic mortals. Possibly they are no less
frequent among those who are not neurotics. Possibly they are part of the
regular store in the—conscious or unconscious—treasury of their memories. But as often as I have been able by means of analysis to bring out a
scene of this sort, it has shown the same peculiarity which startled us with
our present patient too: it has related to *coitus a tergo*, which alone offers
the spectator a possibility of inspecting the genitals. There is surely no
need any longer to doubt that what we are dealing with is only a phantasy,
which is invariably aroused, perhaps, by an observation of the sexual
intercourse of animals." (59).

3. The story of this transferential dynamic is perhaps best told by Peter
Rudnytzky, "Freud's Pompeian Fantasy," in *Reading Freud's Reading*, edited
by Sander Gilman (New York: New York University Press, 1995), 211–31.

4. By far the most interesting treatment of the lizard in Freud's story is
Mary Bergstein's "Gradiva Medica: Freud's Model Female Analyst as
Lizard-Slayer," *American Imago* 60 (2003): 285–301. "Freud," Bergstein
argues, "may have unconsciously overlooked one of his own motivations
for equating Gradiva-Zoe's facility in snaring lizards with her capabilities as
a psychoanalyst. That reason lies in the archeology of the Greco-Roman
world, which is what most attracted Freud to analyze Jensen's novel in the
first place" (292–93). Bergstein's article seeks to describe Freud's contact
with archaeological materials in the years before he wrote his analysis of
Gradiva.

5. Jensen, *Gradiva*, 76.

6. Ibid., 115.

7. Theodor Eimer, *On Orthogenesis: And the Impotence of Natural
Selection in Species Formation*, translated by Thomas J. McCormack
(Chicago: Kegan Paul, 1898), 35. For a review of Eimer's career and an
acute description of the claims of orthogenetics, see Stephen Jay Gould,
The Structure of Evolutionary Theory (Cambridge, Mass.: Harvard
University Press, 2002), 351–96.

8. Jensen, *Gradiva*, 108.

9. Freud, "Delusions and Dreams in Jensen's Gradiva," 54.

10. I do not share the opinion of critics like Zvi Lothane, who read
Freud's analysis of Jensen's *Gradiva* as a record of the Goethian "synthesis
of psychology, art, and literature" that Freud presumably achieved. See his

"The Lessons of a Classic Revisited: Freud on Jensen's *Gradiva*," *Psychoanalytic Review* 97.5 (2010): 789–817. A stronger, more convincing view of the relation between the discursive modes—the disciplines—arranged and embattled in Freud's text may be found in the work of a critic like Geoffrey Hartman, who recently argued that the *Gradiva* essay presents and performs a Hellenistic ideal of what Freud, in a letter to Fliess, calls "form feeling" (*Formgefühl*). For Hartman the discipline of psychoanalysis, in the form of Zoe/Gradiva, embodies and employs *Formgefühl* to lead (figures of) the analysand toward the murky preserves of unacknowledged erotic attachment. I am more sympathetic to this line of interpretation, but Freud's text seems to me much less sure than Hartman—not to mention Lothane—acknowledges that composite figures, whether of the form-feeling sort, of the literature-psychoanalysis sort, or of the animal sort, like an archaeopteryx, are anything but chimeras. See Geoffrey Hartman, "Psychoanalysis as a Cultural Ideal: 'Form Feeling' in Freud's Essay on Gradiva," *American Imago* 65 (2008): 505–22.

DOING IT AS THE BEASTS DID

1. Adam Phillips, *On Flirtation* (Cambridge, Mass.: Harvard University Press, 1996), xii.

2. See Jacques Lezra, *Wild Materialism: The Ethic of Terror and the Modern Republic* (New York: Fordham University Press, 2010).

3. Jacques Derrida, "Archive Fever: A Freudian Impression," translated by Eric Prenowitz, *Diacritics* 25.2 (1995): 54–55.

4. Phillips, *On Flirtation*, xi.

5. Wilhelm Jensen, *Gradiva: Ein pompejanisches Phantasiestück* (Dresden: Carl Reissner, 1903), 145, my translation. " 'Da auf deiner Wange!' Und zugleich schlang der Antwortende plötzlich einen Arm um ihren Nacken und haschte diesmal nach dem von ihm so tief verabscheuten Insekt. . . . Offenbar indes ohne Erfolg, denn gleich danach rief er nochmals: 'Nein, nun sitzt sie dir auf der Lippe!,' und damit wendete er blitzgeschwind seinen Fangversuch dieser zu, jetzt aber so lang ausdauernd, daß kein Zweifel darüber bleiben konnte, er gelange zur vollkommensten Erreichung seines Zweckes."

6. In regard to the gender relations in the story, I would like to come back to Lezra's claim that Zoe, or the pole of the feminine, is identified

with the lizard. Yet at the same time Norbert, as Lezra the Lizard notices, is also identified with the lizard qua the mediating figure of the archaeopteryx. In this scene, however, it appears as if Norbert becomes the lizard who snaps a fly off Zoe's lips. And here I come to "what (Jensen thinks) women want." One might say that this transmission of being-lizard from woman to man is mirrored in the universality of the lizard as a sexual metaphor, which is used for tail-whipping women as well as for the male erect penis in Greek and Latin (*saura, sira*) but also for instance in Caravaggio's *Boy Bitten by a Lizard*. Flirtation, I would argue, relies on this queerness, that is, on the ability of switching between the masculine and the feminine position. Roland Barthes observes in that to the degree that Norbert becomes "feminine" by falling in love, Zoe becomes "masculine" when she restrains her emotions and pretends to be someone else. Roland Barthes, "Gradiva," 1977, in *A Lover's Discourse: Fragments*, translated by Richard Howard (New York: Hill and Wang, 1982), 124–26.

7. John L. Austin, "On Pretending," in *Philosophical Papers*, edited by J. O. Urmson and G. J. Warnock (Oxford: Clarendon, 1970), 204: "On a festive occasion you are ordered, for a forfeit, to pretend to be a hyena: going down on all fours, you make a few essays at hideous laughter and finally bite my calf, taking, with a touch of realism possibly exceeding your hopes, a fair-sized piece right out of it. Beyond question you have gone too far. Try to plead that you were only pretending, and I shall advert forcibly to the state of my calf—not much pretence about that, is there? There are limits, old sport. This sort of thing in these circumstances will not pass as '(only) pretending to be a hyena.' True—but then neither will it pass as *really being* a hyena."

8. Johann Wolfgang Goethe, *The Sorrows of Young Werther*, translated by Burton Pike (New York: Modern Library, 2004), book 2, September 12, 95; Johann Wolfgang Goethe, *Die Leiden des jungen Werther*, edited by Bernt von Heiseler (Bielefeld: Bertelsmann, 1960), 78–79: " 'Er küßt mich auch, sehen Sie!' Als sie dem Tierchen den Mund hinhielt, drückte es sich so lieblich in die süßen Lippen, als wenn es die Seligkeit hätte fühlen können, die es genoß. 'Er soll Sie auch küssen.' Sagte sie und reichte den Vogel herüber.—Das Schnäbelchen machte den Weg von ihrem Munde zu dem meinigen, und die pickende Berührung war wie ein Hauch, eine Ahnung liebevollen Genusses. 'Sein Kuß,' sagte ich, 'ist nicht ganz ohne

Begierde, er sucht Nahrung und kehrt unbefriedigt von der leeren
Liebkosung zurück.' 'Er ißt mir auch aus dem Munde.' Sagte sie.—Sie reicht
ihm einige Brosamen mit ihren Lippen, aus denen die Freuden unschuldig
teilnehmender Liebe in aller Wonne lächelten. Ich kehrte das Gesicht weg.
Sie sollte es nicht tun."

9. Georg Simmel, "Flirtation (1909)," in *On Women, Sexuality, and Love*,
translated and introduction by Guy Oakes (New Haven: Yale University
Press, 1984), 133–52.

10. The feeding of the white bread is another moment that links Lotte to
Zoe: Just as Lotte is cutting bread for her siblings, Zoe, like a mother, is
cutting white bread for the hungry Norbert.

11. Jensen, *Gradiva*, 17, 23, 20.

12. See Emma Barker, "Reading the Greuze Girl—The Daughter's
Seduction," *Representations* 117 (2012): 90. See also Barbara Vinken, who
concentrates on the phallic-erotic connotations of the parrot in her essay
"L'abandon de Félicité—*Un cœur simple* de Flaubert," in *Le Flaubert Réel*,
edited by Barbara Vinken and Peter Fröhlicher (Tübingen: Max Niemeyer,
2009), 153–54.

13. Jensen, *Gradiva*, 7.

14. The lines stem from Mephistopheles in Goethe's *Faust*—"Du
übersinnlicher sinnlicher Freier. Ein Mägdelein nasführet dich" (ll.
3534–35)—and reappear toward the beginning of Leopold von Sacher-
Masoch's *Venus in Furs*, in Gilles Deleuze, *Masochism: Coldness and
Cruelty* (New York: Zone Books, 1991), 151.

CONTRIBUTORS

Sage Anderson is a PhD candidate in the Department of Comparative Literature at New York University and a fellow in the German graduate research group Forms of Knowledge and the Know-how of Living, affiliated with the European University Viadrina, Frankfurt (Oder). She is currently at work on her dissertation, entitled "Life in the Fewest Words: Timing Literary *Brevitas* from *Maximes* to *Denkbilder*."

Rüdiger Campe is a professor of German at Yale University. His books include *Spiel der Wahrscheinlichkeit: Literatur und Berechnung zwischen Pascal und Kleist*, recently translated into English as *The Game of Probability: Literature and Calculation from Pascal to Kleist*, as well as *Affekt und Ausdruck: Zur Umwandlung der literarischen Rede im 17. und 18. Jahrhundert*. He is a recipient of the Humboldt Research Prize and the Aby Warburg Prize and has been a fellow at the Wissenschaftskolleg in Berlin.

Paul Fleming is a professor of Comparative Literature and German at Cornell University and the director of the Institute for German Cultural Studies. He is the author of *The Pleasures of Abandonment: Jean Paul and the Life of Humor* and *Exemplarity and Mediocrity: The Art of the Average from Bourgeois Tragedy to Realism* and has translated books by Peter Szondi and Hans Blumenberg. He is at work on a new project entitled "The Perfect Story," on the literary anecdote.

John Hamilton is a professor of Comparative Literature and German at Harvard University. He is the author of three monographs: *Security: Politics,*

Humanity, and the Philology of Care; *Music, Madness, and the Unworking of Language*; and *Soliciting Darkness: Pindar, Obscurity, and the Classical Tradition*. Hamilton is currently at work on a book project devoted to the philology of the flesh. He has been a fellow at the Wissenschaftskolleg and the Zentrum für Literatur- und Kulturforschung in Berlin.

Arne Höcker is an assistant professor of German at the University of Colorado, Boulder. He is the author of *Epistemologie des Extremen: Lustmord in Kriminologie und Literatur um 1900* and the co-editor of *Wissen. Erzählen. Narrative der Humanwissenschaften* and *Kafkas Institutionen*. He is currently at work on a new project entitled "The Case of Literature: Literary Case Studies from Goethe to Freud."

Daniel Hoffman-Schwartz is an associate research scholar in the Department of Comparative Literature at Princeton University. His work has appeared in the *Oxford Literary Review* and *The Dictionary of Untranslatables*. He is currently at work on his first book, "Infinite Reflection on the Revolution in France: Burke, Theoretical Romanticism, and the Political."

Christophe Koné is visiting assistant professor of German at Williams College. His research focuses on German literature and film, with a particular emphasis on the Weimar period, as well as on issues of gender and sexuality.

Jacques Lezra is a professor of comparative literature, English, German, and Spanish and Portuguese at New York University. His books include *Unspeakable Subjects: The Genealogy of the Event in Early Modern Europe* and *Wild Materialism: The Ethic of Terror and the Modern Republic*. His book *Principles of Insufficient Reason: Mediation and Translation after Marx* is forthcoming. Lezra won the PEN Critical Editions Award for his translation into Spanish of Paul de Man's *Blindness and Insight*.

Barbara Natalie Nagel is an assistant professor in the Department of German at Princeton University. Her first book is *Der Skandal des Literalen: Barocke Literalisierungen in Gryphius, Kleist, Büchner*. She is currently working on a book project entitled "Ambiguous Aggressions: Flirtation,

Passive Aggression, and Domestic Violence in Realism and Beyond." She has published articles in *Law and Literature* and *CLCWeb: Comparative Literature and Culture*.

Lauren Shizuko Stone is a lecturer in the Department of Germanic and Slavic Languages and Literatures at the University of Colorado, Boulder. She is currently preparing her first book, tentatively titled "The 'Small Worlds' of Childhood in Stifter, Rilke, and Benjamin."

Elisabeth Strowick is a professor of German at Johns Hopkins University. She is the author of *Passagen der Wiederholung: Kierkegaard—Lacan—Freud* and *Sprechende Körper—Poetik der Ansteckung: Performativa in Literatur und Rhetorik*. She is currently working on a book entitled " 'Augengespenster'—Studies on the Perception of Reality in 19th-Century German Literature."

Barbara Vinken is a professor of Romance and Comparative Literatures (Allgemeine Literaturwissenschaft und Romanische Philologie) at the Ludwig Maxmilian University in Munich. She has written numerous publications on topics ranging from the Renaissance to contemporary culture; her most recent monographs include *Angezogen: Das Geheimnis der Mode* and *Bestien. Kleist und die Deutschen*.

INDEX

Adorno, Theodor, 7
aesthetics, 2, 4, 6, 8, 9, 18, 21, 28, 30,
    37–38, 44, 49–50, 54, 64–67, 69–70,
    74–75, 107, 111, 120–124, 150n31;
    purposiveness without purpose, 2, 16,
    22, 28, 30. *See also* Kant, Immanuel
Alighieri, Dante, 28
ambiguity, 3, 4, 7, 32, 137
animality, 5, 9, 10, 121–122, 125–142
Aristotle, 7, 45–50, 55, 153n16
Austin, J.L., 8, 75, 77–78, 81, 97, 140,
    158n2, 168n7

Bacon, Francis, 104
Barker, Emma, 142
Barthes, Roland, 4, 7, 22, 150n31, 157n19,
    167n6
Bataille, Georges, 2, 9, 114, 121,
    123
Baudelaire, Charles, 3, 5, 23
Beaton, Cecil, 161n24
Benjamin, Walter, 143n2, 164n3
Bergstein, Mary, 166n4
bestiality, 9–10, 125–142
Binet, Léon, 115
Bloch, Ernst, 2–3, 143n2
body, 16, 28, 38–39, 41, 66, 86–87, 90, 93,
    123, 135. *See also* materiality
Breton, André, 111
Brickman, Cecilia, 164n5
Bronfen, Elisabeth, 145n1
Buchheit, Vincenz, 153n4

Butler, Judith, 8, 62–63

Caillois, Roger, 2, 9, 101–124
Cain, James, 13, 146n16
Campe, Rüdiger, 153n13
capitalism, 3, 6; flirtation as commodity,
    87, 91
Caravaggio, 167n6
Carlyle, Thomas, 89
Cavell, Stanley, 4–6, 13–14, 18, 75, 80–81,
    144nn19,21, 146n15, 158nn1,3,
    159nn5,10
Chandler, Raymond, 13
Cheng, Joyce, 163n10, 165n10
citation, 8, 61–63. *See also* intertextuality
consummation, 15, 62, 116, 126, 136. *See
    also* sex
contingency, 3, 56, 63, 80, 107–108. *See
    also* risk
Copjec, Joan, 145n1
Craigslist, 9, 103–104
Curtius, Ernst Robert, 44

death, 9, 15, 40, 19–20, 94, 104, 105,
    106–108, 115, 116–120, 123–124, 133,
    142, 147n5
De Man, Paul, 146n13
de Vries, Hent, 80–81, 158n3, 160n12
Deleuze, Gilles, 138, 169n14
Delpech, Michel, 84, 160n2
Derrida, Jacques, 69, 72, 75–76, 137,
    145n6, 158n3

 INVENTING WRITING THEORY
Jacques Lezra and Paul North, series editors

Werner Hamacher, *Minima Philologica.* Translated by Catharine Diehl and
Jason Groves

Michal Ben-Naftali, *Chronicle of Separation: On Deconstruction's Disillusioned
Love.* Translated by Mirjam Hadar. Foreword by Avital Ronell

Daniel Hoffman-Schwartz, Barbara Natalie Nagel, and Lauren Shizuko Stone,
eds., *Flirtations: Rhetoric and Aesthetics This Side of Seduction*